THE
BEER GEEK
HANDBOOK

Patrick Dawson

ILLUSTRATED BY *Greg Kletsel*

Storey Publishing

The mission of Storey Publishing is to serve our customers by publishing practical information that encourages personal independence in harmony with the environment.

Edited by Margaret Sutherland and Hannah Fries
Art direction by Jessica Armstrong
Book design and production by Cat Grishaver
Illustrations by © Greg Kletsel

Storey Publishing
210 MASS MoCA Way
North Adams, MA 01247
www.storey.com

Printed in the United States by Versa Press
10 9 8 7 6 5 4 3 2 1

LIBRARY OF CONGRESS CATALOGING-IN-PUBLICATION DATA

Names: Dawson, Patrick, 1982– author. | Kletsel, Greg, illustrator.
Title: The beer geek handbook : living a life ruled by beer / by Patrick
  Dawson ; illustrated by Greg Kletsel.
Description: North Adams, MA : Storey Publishing, [2016]
Identifiers: LCCN 2015050221 | ISBN 9781612125312 (pbk. : alk. paper)
Subjects: LCSH: Beer—Humor. | Beer—Anecdotes.
Classification: LCC PN6231.B43 D39 2016 | DDC 818/.607—dc23 LC record available
  at http://lccn.loc.gov/2015050221

This book is dedicated to craft brewers everywhere — particularly those who make really rare, barrel-aged beer.

Contents

Chapter 5
DRINKING:
WHERE & HOW 127

Chapter 6
THE BEERCATION:
SEEKING THE SOURCE 161

BEER GEEK INITIATION

The natural path for every gluten-tolerant adult should lead them to falling in love with beer. This wonderful result of hops, malt, yeast, and water can produce some of life's finest sensory pleasures, flooding the brain, tongue, and olfactory system with waves of enjoyment. For decades, however, the makers of watered-down factory lagers slowly brainwashed the general public into thinking that beer was just a cheap, semi-palatable way for the masses to achieve drunkenness.

Fortunately, that time has passed, and a new era, full of discovery, creativity, and excitement, has dawned over this incredible beverage. There is no better time than the present to explore and enjoy beer, and anybody with a functioning liver would do themselves a disservice not to take the first steps of the journey to becoming a full-fledged Beer Geek.

Within these pages lies all you need to be safely guided down the path of enlightenment. Even the most veteran beer connoisseur will find valuable knowledge here: how to flawlessly pull off a beer tasting, talk shop with the worst of beery know-it-alls, understand the proper etiquette of bottle shares, gracefully correct uninformed bartenders, and more — all in single-serving portions so you can take it in without getting tipsy. Most importantly, you'll be able to pull off all of this while coming across as an activist for beer, rather than a snob.

So stop being intimidated by the burgeoning beer scene simply because you don't know what a firkin is or how to pronounce *gueuze*. While all Beer Geeks give the impression of being weaned on imperial stouts, their first (and many subsequent) beers were almost certainly of the "lite" variety too. We all have to learn to wade into the deep end . . . and you now hold in your hands the perfect floatie.

CHAPTER 1
BEER GEEKS

AN INTRODUCTION

To a Beer Geek, beer is not simply something to drink, but a lifestyle. Just as tennis players would never consider their sport simply exercise, or sports-car buffs view a Ferrari as mere transportation, Beer Geeks see beer not as a means to get drunk but as something to be analyzed, researched, discussed, photographed, cataloged, and then, finally, consumed (see the first Beer Geek Commandment, page 13). Beer books fill their shelves, rare glassware is displayed proudly, and pennies are pinched to save up for a trip to Belgium.

WHILE YOUR UNCLE ROY can immediately tell you that his favorite beer is Bud Light, when asked the same question a Beer Geek will struggle, asking qualifiers like country of origin, applicable weather, hop content, and sessionability before eventually settling on 12 definitive answers with an accompanying flow chart. Beer seeps into all aspects of life, resulting in dogs named Hunahpu and children named Simcoe.

BEER GEEKS
BY REGION

PACIFIC NORTHWESTERN BEER GEEK
Whether it's felling timber or slaying **whales** (rare beers), the Jacks and Jills of the PacNW always bring it.

MIDWESTERN BEER GEEK
The midwestern Beer Geek knows the value of hard work and uses it to promote the region's brews to epic proportions.

SOUTHERN BEER GEEK
The fearless southern Beer Geek would wrestle an alligator for that rare one-off DIPA.

NEW ENGLAND BEER GEEK

This hardy sort survives the brutal nor'easters with the help of the region's juicy, tropical IPAs.

ROCKY MOUNTAIN BEER GEEK

After shredding the slopes, only the finest **session beers** will do for this outdoorsy breed.

CALIFORNIA BEER GEEK

This relaxed, ocean-loving variety is particularly adept at whale spotting (and drinking).

THE GEEK AND THE SNOB

IT IS IMPORTANT TO UNDERSTAND that not all who obsess over beer are Beer Geeks. A fine but definitive line exists in the beery arena that separates the Beer Geeks from the Beer Snobs. While Beer Geeks will give the impression of knowing all (and not recalling a time when they didn't), they don't gloat or impose their knowledge like Beer Snobs do. Information is given gladly, but never in a condescending fashion.

Additionally, although the world of beer certainly has its specialized lingo (see The Beer Geek Dictionary, page 188), when a Beer Snob tries to impress the uninitiated with highfalutin language it only serves to isolate. Beer Geeks, on the other hand, learn to effortlessly tailor their vocabulary to the geekiness level of the person to whom they are speaking. For example, if you asked veteran Beer Geeks if they wanted a pour of "CBS," they would immediately know that you are referring to Founder's Brewing Breakfast Stout that has been aged in used maple syrup bourbon barrels. If asking a non–Beer Geek the same question, you'd instead simply ask if they wanted to try a "strong stout." A Beer Geek is aware that the beer will speak for itself. If the non–Beer Geek enjoys it (and they damn well better — it is CBS for crying out loud), a Beer Geek will use the opportunity to explain that it was aged in whiskey barrels, how that lends a vanilla-like presence, and so on.

To a Beer Geek, the more beer activism in the world, the better a place it will be.

To a Beer Snob, beer knowledge is something to be hoarded, and pulled out only to put a newbie in his place. A Beer Geek uses that same knowledge to show the uninitiated the light.

This all stems from a shared understanding within the Beer Geek community. Call it a list of commandments, if you will. This value system of sorts is something of an unspoken code, never really discussed but rather absorbed through interaction with fellow Beer Geeks, internet forums, and the like. Veteran Beer Geeks would have a hard time verbalizing them if pressed, but these tenets are second nature, like always serving a barleywine in a snifter.

THE BEER GEEK TEN COMMANDMENTS

— I —

Beer is something to be understood, appreciated, and analyzed, not just a means to get drunk.

An intimate understanding of the various styles of beer is a must for all Beer Geeks. Before even drinking a beer, they already have a certain amount of knowledge that allows them to develop an expectation from which they can more deeply analyze the beer. When drinking, the aroma and taste of a beer are evaluated constantly, but not without pleasure. Their breadth of expertise and experience would allow them to easily write a 500-word review of a 1-ounce sample of beer. Taking tasting notes at a bar is a normal thing. Without thinking it odd, a Beer Geek uses the terms *horse blanket* and *cob webs* when describing a beer.

— II —

A Beer Geek sees it as his duty to (tastefully) inform the world about the joys of beer.

While Beer Geeks may take pride in their skill and proficiency, they aren't apt to flaunt it. Instead, they parse wisdom when necessary to correct a situation (such as a bar using frozen mugs), or when they see an opportunity to encourage a burgeoning beer lover. It's not unusual for them to be mistaken as an employee at their favorite liquor store, or even to have the store's beer buyer ask their advice. An act as simple as stopping a guy from buying bottled Heineken — and letting him know that the canned version won't have the dreaded "skunky" flavor — might very well bring another convert into the ranks of Beer Geek.

— III —

A Beer Geek is not cheap, at least when it comes to beer.

Unfortunately, good beer often comes at a premium, and some degree of dispos-able income is required to fully revel in the Beer Geek lifestyle. If circumstances dictate that your disposable income has to come from eating ramen alongside your vintage Cantillon gueuze, so be it. A Beer Geek has surely had at least one three-digit liquor store purchase and has probably used the word *bargain* when describing certain beers over twenty dollars. Money is still used wisely, though, and metrics like dollars-per-ounce are applied when considering beer purchases.

— IV —

A Beer Geek understands brewing techniques.

To properly evaluate the end product, a Beer Geek relies on his understanding of the various processes used to create beer. For example, knowing the differ-ence between a turbid and a single infusion mash enables one to recognize that the former will retain a superior **mouthfeel** if cellared. And if that sentence made no sense, beyond making you chuckle at the word *mouthfeel*, have no fear; we'll make a Beer Geek out of you yet.

— V —

A Beer Geek shares her beer freely, regardless of its rarity or her audience.

While Beer Geeks are certainly enticed by the rarity of a bottle, they also under-stand that it's a product that ultimately begs to be enjoyed. The Beer Geek community is one of sharing and generosity, where bottle shares are common and nothing (well, except for *that one* bottle . . .) is held back. In the spirit of converting the enthusiastic, Beer Geeks will happily open a whale for those who might appreciate it.

— VI —
A Beer Geek has a beer cellar.

Whether it's the crisper drawer of a refrigerator or a 2,000-bottle offsite storage unit, a Beer Geek recognizes that beer is a time-sensitive product that sometimes requires a month or a decade to mature. Potential domiciles are carefully evaluated for their beer storage and temperature control capabilities.

— VII —
A Beer Geek's travel plans revolve around beer.

Beer-centric vacations (beercations) — focused on visiting breweries, bars, and general regions that specialize in sought-after beer — are the norm. Beer is always brought back for in-home consumption and sharing, and a Beer Geek is intimately familiar with an airline's baggage policy. To facilitate hotel-room quaffing (and expand drinking time), a Beer Geek typically travels with a tulip glass.

— VIII —
A Beer Geek is part of the local beer community.

There is a social aspect to being a Beer Geek. Attending tastings, frequenting brewery taprooms, camping outside of liquor stores, etc. not only permit a Beer Geek to stay in the loop of local happenings, but also provide opportunities to share knowledge of the latest beery news. Inevitably, a Beer Geek's circle of friends will be made up of fellow Beer Geeks.

— IX —
A Beer Geek has a vast understanding of regional distribution systems.

Budding Beer Geeks quickly realize that the best and most-desired beer happens to be that which is not distributed to one's home state. It is essential that Beer Geeks know which breweries are in their local beer distribution system, but also the distribution portfolio of other areas so they can best determine how to acquire that must-have beer.

— X —
A Beer Geek keeps up on the pulse of the beer scene.

The craft beer scene changes rapidly, and one must stay vigilant to keep informed. In addition to being locally involved, a Beer Geek regularly cruises internet beer forums, follows breweries' social media feeds, maintains beer magazine subscriptions, and reads the latest beer books. A month or two out of touch will cause a Beer Geek to miss out on limited releases or epic tappings, causing a downward spiral that will surely lead to misery and desolation.

THE BEER MENU

While Beer Geeks love their brews, they're also stewards of the craft and, as such, have a responsibility to enlighten those less fortunate than themselves. The following scenarios are designed to help clarify some of the finer points of Beer Geekery when it comes to interacting with non-geeks.

1. You're on your way to a ball game with some friends. After parking a mile away in an effort to save a couple bucks, you decide to pop into a neighborhood pub for a quick round. Saddling up to the bar, you're confronted with the following. Which do you choose?

a. Some "lite" beer, the best low-calorie horse piss advertising can brainwash you to buy.

b. Corona, the beer that requires the addition of mouth-puckering citrus to become even semi-palatable.

c. Bottled Heineken; skunkiness is a good thing, right?

d. Politely decline and ask for water.

2. Your friend is throwing a big BBQ bash for his birthday. You show up and after you hand the host his gift, he pops open the cooler and asks what you'd like to drink. With a quick survey of the following, which do you choose?

a. PBR, the host's favorite.

b. Keystone Light, his second favorite.

c. Fosters, his attempt at pleasing the Beer Geeks.

d. Politely decline and ask for water.

3. You're heading to your annual family get-together and your aunt has asked everyone to bring beer or wine to share. After swinging by your favorite bottle shop, what six-pack is buckled safely into your dedicated beer car seat?

a. Rolling Rock; it may taste like canned corn juice, but your uncles love it.

b. Sierra Nevada Pale Ale, the hoppy yet balanced classic.

c. New Belgium Rampant; if they don't like this 85 IBU bruiser of a double IPA, more for you!

d. Allagash White; fruity, wheaty, with a hint of spice, these go down dangerously easy.

NOITCUDORTNI NA ,SKEEG REEB

ANSWERS

1. **D**, or even better, order a bourbon (it's just a super-concentrated oak-aged barleywine, after all). A Beer Geek won't waste their hard-earned cash on a pint of something they don't like. Plus, by civilly declining their beer choices, a Beer Geek is subtly encouraging the bar to expand their options, potentially aiding the next Beer Geek who happens to walk in.

2. **A**, **B**, or **C**; choose your poison. While you can certainly send a message when spending your own money, it's entirely inappropriate to do the same when being hosted at someone's place. Be a Beer Geek, not a Beer Snob. After all, your host likely knows you're crazy about beer and will be embarrassed if you opt for anything else.

3. **B** & **D**. There was a time when even you hadn't seen the light. Look at this as an opportunity to pay it forward and educate your family with some great "gateway" craft beers. Pairing the Sierra Nevada's spicy yet sensible hoppiness with some food or enjoying the intriguing yet pleasing flavor profile of the Allagash White might just convince your cousin Larry to ditch the Lime-A-Rita.

BEER DRINKERS
COMMONLY CONFUSED WITH
BEER GEEKS

BEER GEEKS DON'T TYPICALLY FIT into an easily recognizable mold, at least not in a physical sense. They come in skinny, rotund, old, and young. Outside of a Toppling Goliath shirt or a BREW OR DIE tattoo, there are not many ways to pick them out of a crowd. Instead, behavioral cues based on the Beer Geek Ten Commandments will tip you off to a person's affinity for fancy suds.

Unsurprisingly, the non–Beer Geek populous often mistakenly thinks that anybody who drinks great amounts of craft beer is automatically a Beer Geek. Meet the usual suspects . . .

GRANOLA JUNKIE · FOODIE · CRAFT DRUNK · OLD GUY · THE TICKER · BEER HIPSTER

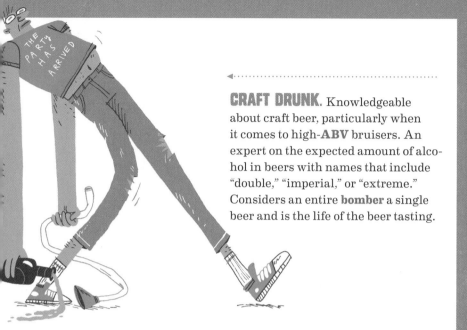

CRAFT DRUNK. Knowledgeable about craft beer, particularly when it comes to high-**ABV** bruisers. An expert on the expected amount of alcohol in beers with names that include "double," "imperial," or "extreme." Considers an entire **bomber** a single beer and is the life of the beer tasting.

TICKER. If it ain't rare, it doesn't exist. The Ticker's only desire is to obtain and display the most hyped, rare beer. Once the beer has been drunk, there is no point in ever trying it again (hence the name, as the beer has been "ticked" off a list). Frequently posts beer "haul" photos on social media sites and makes snide remarks on beer trading websites. Has never drunk a Sierra Nevada Pale Ale. Also, often a Glass Snob (see Glassware: Always a Proper Vessel on page 40).

THE OLD GUY. Fell in love with craft beer during the '90s brewery boom and still refers to all craft beer as either "microbrews" or "imports." Avoids overly hoppy or funky beers but has a deep appreciation for the Euro classics. Has a best friend who used to own or work at a brewery, usually Charlie Papazian or Larry Bell. Often seen at chain brewpubs drinking mugs of kolsch and wearing a Pete's Wicked Ale T-shirt.

THE FOODIE. Has a profound love of culinary adjectives. Does not eat vanilla pudding but rather French-made, hand-curdled blancmange made from heirloom miniature Dutch cow milk. Applies same gusto to beers. Asks unsuspecting servers ingredient-sourcing questions such as *Did they use whole leaf hibiscus in this saison? Is the coffee in this stout shade-grown? Tell me about the upbringing of these New Zealand hops . . .*

BEER HIPSTER. Longing for nostalgia (and broke from buying hundred-dollar hand-stenciled neck scarves), the average hipster often opts for retro-labeled canned adjunct lagers (perhaps not knowing they're just rebranded and brewed by industrial conglomerates). Identified by their combination of a waxed moustache and an affinity for beers or breweries with literary names (preferably nineteenth-century Russian authors).

GRANOLA JUNKIE. Loves mountain-centric activities (hiking, skiing, biking) and beer. Opts for breweries that have at least one collaboration beer with a musician whose apparel portfolio includes tie-dye (preferably a bluegrass or jam band musician). Prefers low-ABV, balanced beers that lend themselves to activity-based imbibing.

ARE YOU A BEER GEEK?

Check *yes* or *no* to indicate whether the following apply to you. Total your *yes* responses to see how much of a Beer Geek you already are.

YES   **NO**   *Have you ever . . .*

☐ ☐ **1.** been caught swirling and sniffing a glass of tap water prior to drinking it?

☐ ☐ **2.** brought your own glass to a beer tasting?

☐ ☐ **3.** transferred your beer from a pint glass to a wine glass while at a bar?

☐ ☐ **4.** provided beer suggestions to a stranger at a liquor store?

☐ ☐ **5.** had a liquor store set beer aside for you without asking?

☐ ☐ **6.** been on a beercation?

☐ ☐ **7.** flown Southwest purely because of their "two free bags" policy (both of yours were cases of beer)?

☐ ☐ **8.** camped outside a brewery or liquor store?

☐ ☐ **9.** asked what vintage a beer is?

☐ ☐ **10.** hosted a "cellar cleaning" party and genuinely hoped that people didn't bring more beer?

☐ ☐ **11.** used the term barnyard to describe a beer you enjoyed?

☐ ☐ **12.** worn two pairs of pants on the plane to make more room for beer in your luggage?

YES **NO**

☐ ☐ **13.** given a cellar-worthy beer as a baby-shower present with instructions for it to be opened on the kid's 21st birthday.

☐ ☐ **14.** returned a beer served in a frozen glass, along with an explanation of the temperature-sensitive nature of aromatic hop oils and yeast esters?

☐ ☐ **15.** called someone by their BeerAdvocate.com or RateBeer.com username?

Do you . . .

☐ ☐ **16.** know who Tomme Arthur is?

☐ ☐ **17.** know the difference between hoppy and bitter?

☐ ☐ **18.** have a beer cellar?

☐ ☐ **19.** know what the acronym ISO stands for?

☐ ☐ **20.** have the number of your store's beer guy saved in your phone?

♥ **MORE THAN 16:** *Beer Geek. You are to be esteemed and congratulated. Keep reading.*

♥ **BETWEEN 11 AND 15:** *Beer Enthusiast. Almost there, but keep reading.*

♥ **FEWER THAN 10:** *Keep reading.*

NUMBER OF YES ANSWERS?

CHAPTER 2
BEER
THE ROOT OF ALL
BEER GEEKERY

It's easy to get lost in the hoopla of beer trading, one-off releases, and beard-grooming techniques, but in the end, being a Beer Geek is really about a deep, unnatural love for beer. A love that transcends class, race, and sex and can only be completely understood by others who have seen that perfectly opaque, lightly carbonated golden light.

SINCE THE TIME OF THE ANCIENT SUMERIANS, humans have appreciated the result of fermented barley or, as we call it, beer. Way back then, it provided the multiple benefits of sanitizing drinking water, delivering sustenance, and taking the edge off after a long day of creating civilization. In short, the world as we know it wouldn't exist if it weren't for our forebearers' affinity for earthen mugs of ale.

Beer has been on a long journey ever since. From the first hopped beers in the ninth century to the barleywines of 1800s England, this sweet nectar has been gradually tweaked to match the tastes and ingredients of different cultures. In the globalized information era we live in today, though, brewers are only limited by their imaginations, and beer drinkers have responded enthusiastically, to say the least. Beer is making a strong case for the world's drink of choice, and Beer Geeks are banging the rally drum for all to hear.

THE
IDEAL BEER

WHAT DOES A BEER GEEK LOOK FOR in a beer? This is a complex question to answer, and every adored beer has a slightly different story. A common set of characteristics seems to surface among such beers, however, painting a picture of what it takes to brew Beer Geek gold.

AROMA: A beer must provide an aromatic experience. Beer Geeks savor their beer and get almost as much satisfaction from smelling it as drinking it.

BREWER CREDENTIALS *(optional)*: Most Beer Geeks pride themselves on being able to appreciate a good beer regardless of its producer. However, knowing a beer is made by a fellow Beer Geek makes it that much more enjoyable.

MOUTHFEEL: An IPA may be delicious and smell like a hop field in bloom, but if it has the body of club soda, the experience is ruined. Mouthfeel completes the package.

COMPLEXITY *(optional)*: A Beer Geek may love the simple, acrid nature of a coffee stout. But to make her heart sing, barrel-age that same stout to add flavors of vanilla, caramel, and coconut.

TASTE: A beer must taste good.

BREWING METHOD: Beer Geeks pour their hearts and souls into their enjoyment of beer and expect the people who make it to have the same attitude when brewing. Beer Geeks thrive on learning and appreciating the work that goes into their brews, and therefore frown greatly on shortcuts.

RARITY *(optional)*: A beer doesn't have to be difficult to acquire, but damned if that doesn't make everything taste better.

THE IMPORTANCE OF
KNOWING (AND IGNORING)
BEER STYLES

To TRULY LOVE BEER, a Beer Geek needs to *know* beer, and not just that it's made from barley and hops. One needs to understand the entire spectrum of types and their nuances. For example, a classic mistake of a **noob** (a somewhat derogatory term for one who has not reached Beer Geekdom) is to downplay pilsners, grouping them all in with the mass-produced American factory lagers. But a Beer Geek knows the bliss that can come from the floral hops and crisp, carbonic bite of a Weihenstephaner Pilsner. A firm knowledge of the subtleties that differentiate styles allows Beer Geeks to set an expectation for the beer before tasting it, enabling them to maximize the quality of their analysis and subsequent enjoyment (or critique).

The guidelines for beer styles are laid out and defined by two different governing bodies: the Beer Judge Certification Program (BJCP) and the Brewers Association. These two generally tend to agree, though the BJCP guidelines are typically more comprehensive while the strength of the Brewers Association guidelines is that they are updated more frequently and therefore include newly emerging styles (**Brett** IPAs, for example). For the most part, the guidelines were created for the sake of beer competitions so that beers could be judged against similar counterparts, but they are also used by brewers who design beers.

The style guidelines are written, reviewed, and maintained by an assembly of beer "experts" (historians, brewers, writers, drunks, etc.) who use their combined wealth of experience to come to a consensus on what characterizes a specific style of beer. The guidelines include a description of the expected appearance, aroma, taste, mouthfeel, and overall impression of the beer. Along with the descriptions, there are quantified specifics like IBU range, final gravity, color, and ABV. Since these guidelines are designed to aid brewers in designing beers, also included is information on typical or acceptable ingredients, as well as any historically significant brewing techniques (such as decoction mashing of a bock).

While no Beer Geek will argue the importance of being aware of and understanding the guidelines, many will debate their usefulness. Some say that using them to critique a beer is shortsighted, that they are arbitrary constraints that hamper creativity. The opposing side, the style tyrants, reply that the guidelines are critical, time-tested outlines that lead brewers toward creating the ideal beer.

Here's an example: You head to your local brewery and order their Belgian wit. By definition, the beer should have a honey-like sweetness, peppery phenols, citrusy esters, and little to no hop presence. This beer has all those things in spades, except it's got this intense tropical fruitiness from being dry hopped, which you find delicious. The fact that it misses the hoppy aspect of the style guidelines does not make it a bad beer — far from it. But style tyrants would disagree and dismiss it as being "not to style."

Most Beer Geeks know that the truth lies somewhere in between. Style guidelines are viewed as base knowledge. Just as a chef should first know how to cook a basic pot roast before working on their braised, alder-smoked beef cheek recipe, brewers should learn how to brew the classics before looking to color outside the lines.

A Beer Geek has an appreciation for the basic beer styles and can use them as tools for comparison, but judges beers based on their merits, not necessarily their compliance with the guidelines.

What's in a Name?

PROBABLY THE BIGGEST ISSUE concerning styles is in their proper usage (or lack thereof) when naming a beer. Some breweries are reluctant to note a style on their labels for one reason or another — fear of style tyrants, being too cool to be pigeonholed by such things, etc. — and instead they use some random nonsensical name. (Evil Twin Brewing is one of the worst offenders. With names like Even More Jesus or Ryan and the Beaster Bunny, it's anybody's guess as to whether you're buying an imperial stout, an IPA, or the demo tape of a bad '90s band.) This puts beer consumers in a predicament, not knowing exactly what they're getting into when making a purchase. Equally bad is finding some suggestion of a style, but it's too generic, à la Upslope Brewing Company's Craft Lager. This name is quite possibly the most infuriating one ever conjured, the equivalent of a restaurant menu featuring a dish called "Meat with an Assortment of Things."

Other times, though, a simple style name is not enough. For example, if a brewery labels their coffee-infused, tequila barrel–aged IPA just as an IPA, they're not being fair to the consumer. Beer drinkers have the right to more information so they can avoid this beer with all their being.

BEER TYPES
THE GOOD, THE BAD, THE TRENDY

AGAIN, THE FOUNDATION of Beer Geekery is a solid understanding of the basic beer styles. Here is a CliffsNotes version of their general characteristics and current Beer Geek attitudes toward them:

LIGHT LAGER. Often dismissed due to its inclusion of the "lite" American lager, this category also consists of such great beers as the Munich helles and the Dortmunder export. Sweet, but not **cloying**, with a subtle hop bitterness, the incredible drinkability of these two styles proves this is a category to be reckoned with. You're not a Beer Geek until you've drunk a **Maß** (one-liter mug) of Spaten helles while eating some sort of tubed pork meat.

PILSNER. Made up of three different varieties: the German pilsner, best known for its dry finish and high bitterness due to the local sulfate-rich water; the Czech pilsner, maltier than its German cousin and with a spicy hop bite from the local Saaz hops; and the American pilsner, a near-extinct style that early US brewers made with corn and American hops — rich and hoppy, Budweiser this is not. With nowhere in this beer for flaws to hide, Beer Geeks respect the extreme care brewers have to take to create this light, quaffable brew.

EUROPEAN AMBER LAGER. Oktoberfest beers for the most part, but also includes the Vienna lager, a delicately malty amber with an elegant, dry finish. However, with so many bad versions of this style (*ahem*, Negra Modelo), it's an easy category to dump on. Still, anyone who has had the excellent German-brewed versions of these beers realizes there is no better showcase of the kilned Munich and Vienna malts.

BOCK. While not a hugely common or popular style in the United States, the intensely malt-rich bocks deserve more attention than they get. Made by **decoction mashing** (repeatedly boiling **wort** to kettle-caramelize the malt), these beers are considered by many to be too sweet, which is no surprise considering the most popular — the extra-strength dopplebock — was created to give sustenance to fasting monks. Which leads to the logical conclusion of many Beer Geeks that one should crack a bottle of Paulaner Salvator every Sunday morning for spiritual guidance.

HYBRID BEER. Called hybrid because they could be made with either ale or lager yeasts, the "light" beers of this category includes such American beer staples as the wheat and blonde ales. Not a whole lot for Beer Geeks to get excited about. The amber hybrids are similar but with a little roasted malt and include the German altbier and the common (steam) ale. In general, hybrids are viewed as nothing more than BBQ beers.

....

ENGLISH PALE ALE. These are the beers that started the US microbrew craze and the same beers that no one seems to care about anymore. They include beers like Fuller's ESB (Extra Special Bitter) and Boddington's Pub Ale. Malty, medium-strength, and made with UK-produced hops, they now come off as a bit flat and unexciting when compared to today's hoppier, cleaner American ales. Kind of like a Sega Genesis compared to the PlayStation 4. There's some fun nostalgia there, but there's really no going back.

SCOTTISH AND IRISH ALE. Includes traditional Scottish ales, Irish red ales, and wee heavy ales. Malty, sometimes with a hint of peat, these beers have little to no hop presence. This stems from the high taxation and logistical difficulties involved with importing hops from the UK (they don't grow well in cool Scotland). That and the Scottish disdain for all things British. Not terribly popular anymore, except for the wee heavy ale whose bruising strength speaks to Beer Geeks' penchant for high ABV beers.

AMERICAN ALE. The general category for general styles: American pale ale, American brown ale, and American amber ale. Basically, take the English version of these and make them cleaner (yeast-wise, with fewer esters and no diacetyl) and substantially hoppier. While the style guidelines define the expected hoppiness and ABV of these beers, they are always changing, and usually in an upward direction. These are the session ales of the Beer Geeks, and their profiles are constantly tweaked to match ever-changing tastes.

A Session on Sessions

SESSION **IS ONE OF THE MOST USED** and beloved adjectives of a Beer Geek. The word is generally used to describe a beer that can be consumed in relatively large volumes over a long drinking session. Session beers are first and foremost low in alcohol. Some say the cutoff is 5% ABV, while others argue 4.5%. (This seemingly menial difference of opinion will lead some Beer Geeks to come to blows. Beer-fueled passion is an interesting thing.) These beers should also have a low amount of residual sugars (think "lite" beer) and a flavor profile that won't wear out your palate. Not overly bitter, roasted, sour, or anything else, they are great beers to consume while watching sporting events, BBQing, or supervising children.

IPA (INDIA PALE ALE). First created by the English in the nineteenth century, IPAs were brewed with more hops and had a higher ABV than the traditional pale ales. This allowed them to better survive the long trip to troops stationed in India. Fast-forward to today, and the beers that bear this name have only the slightest resemblance to those initial pioneering ales. Now made with ridiculous amounts of hops and even more alcohol, they've grown to represent the evolved tastes of the American Beer Geek. Every few years you'll find new and creative takes on this style, with the latest fueled by the intensely fruity experimental hops being bred in hop labs around the world. Big-time Beer Geek beers.

DOUBLE IPA. Beer Geeks love IPAs. And in the spirit of American ingenuity, it follows that what makes something good (i.e., hops) could be doubled to make it great. Double IPAs (DIPAs) have more hops, more malts, and more alcohol than their predecessor.

If an IPA were an SUV, a DIPA would be a monster truck driven by a deranged, drunken Kool-Aid Man.

The development of the DIPA has followed a similar path as the IPA, with an ever-increasing amount of hoppiness and experimentation with new flavors stemming from the new school of experimental hops.

GERMAN WHEAT BEER. Essentially hefeweizens (and their obscure darker counterparts, the dunkelweizen and weizenbock), these beers saw ridiculous extremes in popularity back in the early 2000s. A unique flavor combination of banana and cloves along with a fluffy body make for a very distinctive beer experience. Particularly popular among sorority girls and German sheepherders, the German wheat beer is currently in vogue as something to dislike, but it's enjoying a quiet resurgence among purist Beer Geeks.

BELGIAN AND FRENCH ALES. A very broad category that encompasses Belgian wit beer, saison, and bière de garde. From the realm of traditional Belgian brewers and Americans with a fondness for using words such as *artisanal, rustic, farmhouse,* and *handmade,* these ales are made with unruly yeast strains and a variety of unusual grains and ingredients. When done correctly, these can be some of the finest beers in the world, giving a talented brewer the ability to showcase unique ingredients. For the same reason they earn high praise in the Beer Geek world. However, since these beers are notoriously hard to define, many beers that aren't really saisons — but are too yeasty or turbid to be called anything else — get a *saison* label slapped on them and are sold for a premium. Buyer beware.

SOUR ALE. A collection of beers spanning from tart to mouth-puckeringly acidic. Includes the Berliner weisse, a lightly tart German wheat beer; the Flanders red ale, a fruity, almost winelike, oak-aged ale; and lambic, the spontaneously fermented, blended wild Belgian wheat ale. In the early 2010s Beer Geeks dragged this style up from the ashes like a phoenix. Tired of the limitations of traditional yeasts and their flavors, they flocked to the seemingly endless array of flavors that can be derived in these styles. Sour ales are sometimes made with fruits and are typically brewed in small batches, driving up both the price and the Beer Geek's heart rate.

AMERICAN WILD ALE. As Beer Geeks began to discover and obsess over the sour beers of Europe, US breweries responded with their own versions. After all, most brewers are Beer Geeks themselves. A new wave of beers that were often sour but sometimes just a little funky (or wild) hit the scene, with very mixed results. This new breed of ales didn't quite fit the mold of its European counterparts. Often, they were made with different ingredients, brewed untraditionally, and inoculated with cultured "wild" yeast (the horror!). Some incredibly creative soul decided they would be called American Wild Ales, and this worthless moniker has stuck. The style seemingly encompasses any beer from stouts to saisons brewed with *Brettanomyces* yeast or souring bacteria, and trying to group all of them into a single generic category has proved rather silly. Regardless, the best in the group have shone through and captured a place in Beer Geeks' hearts.

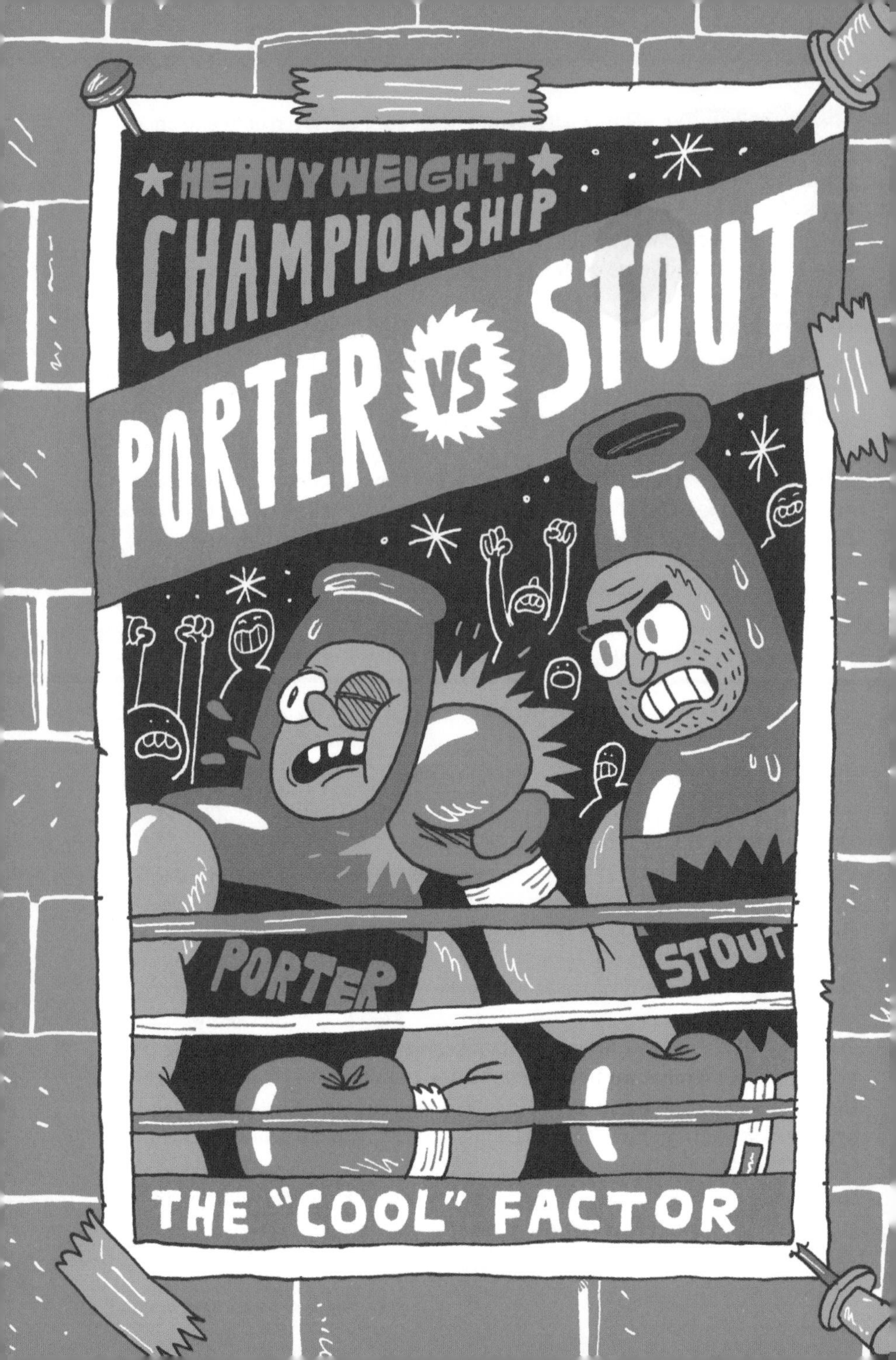
HEAVYWEIGHT
CHAMPIONSHIP
PORTER VS STOUT
PORTER
STOUT
THE "COOL" FACTOR

PORTER. Dark, malty beers with roasted notes ranging from coffee to chocolate. Considered a bit more of an old-school style, porters received a popularity boost by Beer Geek darling Hill Farmstead, whose flagship beer, Everett, happens to be a porter. This brewery, which will set most Beer Geeks to dry humping the nearest piece of furniture, helped elevate this humble style back into Beer Geek grace.

STOUT. Often one of the gateway beers for burgeoning Beer Geeks who are most familiar with fizzy, yellow lagers; many are shocked and strangely excited about drinking something so dark and full of flavor that they're used to finding in a coffee mug. There is a huge variety of stout types too, ranging from the hoppy American stout to the dry Irish version, not to mention the powerhouse imperial stout. The intense roasted flavors lend themselves to a variety of creative additions, such as coffee, bourbon, vanilla, coconut, ham hocks, and more, making it a Beer Geek staple.

Porter vs. Stout

BEER GEEKS ARE REPRESENTATIVES of the beer world and thus are often asked the same questions by non–Beer Geeks. A classic example is how a porter and a stout differ, since both are near-black and dominated by roasted malt flavor. The answer is *not a whole helluva lot*. While beers in the upper end of the stout spectrum are often more roasted and slightly higher in alcohol than porters are, there is a gray area where both of these beers exist. In fact, many of the beers made in the United States that are called stouts would really be better described as porters. Since "stout" is an inherently cooler name, however, it gets used more often.

BELGIAN STRONG ALE. Traditionally, Belgians aren't fond of categorizing beers and find American Beer Geeks' insistence on doing it somewhere on the border of amusing and annoying. It's been a challenge for Beer Geeks to try to define Belgian styles, as the Belgians seem to create every sort of random, odd beer imaginable and not follow many rules. For this reason, the category encompasses Belgian blondes, dubbels, tripels, and the ever-descriptive strong Belgian golden ale and strong Belgian dark ale.

A very wide range of profiles appears within these types. However, seeing as they are almost always high in alcohol, flavor-forward, and made in a country other than the United States, they've found the recipe for high popularity in the Beer Geek scene.

STRONG ALE. The domain of American and English barleywines, two somewhat similar beers, with the English being more malty and yeasty and the American version tending to have more hop bitterness/flavor/aroma. They are very high in alcohol (10–18% ABV), which not only makes for some intense beers but also suits them well for barrel aging and home cellaring — two magical terms to a Beer Geek. Very highly regarded.

Beer Judging

BEER COMPETITIONS are everywhere, and any beer event worth its salt uses certified beer judges (a surprising number use random beer drinkers, any of whose palate may be on par with that of a chain-smoking monkey). The typical path to becoming a legit beer judge is to go through the aptly named Beer Judge Certification Program, which involves both written and sensory tests. By excelling at those tests and logging hours at competitions, judges can rise through the ranks: first Apprentice, then Certified, and finally something like Purple Level III Grand Master (the rank names seem to be heavily inspired by Dungeons & Dragons). Attaining a higher rank will earn a judge a shiny pin that she can lord over lowly apprentice judges who dare contradict her evaluation.

Judging presents a bit of a quandary at first, since you must judge a beer not simply on how good it is but also on how it measures up in its style category. Even so, beer judging can be a fantastic thing. There is no better process to sharpen and broaden your palate than to have to write a small essay describing a beer. However, a Beer Geek doesn't lose sight of enjoying a beer for what it is, thus avoiding that slippery slope to becoming a style tyrant.

GLASSWARE
ALWAYS A PROPER VESSEL

THE BELGIANS don't take much seriously. They certainly create and enjoy some of the world's best beers, but they don't have an ultra-solemn attitude about it all. To them, while a beer must be good and must be paired with the right food and mood, the vast majority of the population hasn't reached the point of making it a lifestyle. Which is precisely why it's peculiar that Belgians are so very fanatical about their glassware.

Go to a bar in Brussels and nearly every beer has its own dedicated glass. From a distance, the collection of goblets and tulips is almost overwhelming, making it look more like a Waterford Crystal museum than what it actually is . . . a place to look like a fool trying to pronounce *gueuze* (see page 191, Commonly Mispronounced Beer Names and Terms).

The legend goes that each beer's glass has been designed to perfectly complement the nuances of that specific beer. The curvature of the glass creates the perfect head retention, the diameter lets in the exact amount of light for the idyllic hue, the arc of lip flawlessly spreads the beer across the ideal receptors on your tongue, and so on. And while some of this might be true, the fact is that much of the Belgium beer glass scene is actually about marketing. American beer bars have neon signs proclaiming what's being poured, while Belgian bars take the more civilized approach of having their vast array of glasses do the work.

While Beer Geeks understand that much of the hubbub around glassware is marketing hype, they don't jump to the conclusion that we should be barbarians and drink all beer out of pint glasses.

No, glass type and shape is important to Beer Geeks, but having a glass for every single beer is viewed by *most* as a bit over the top.

IONIC

TULIP

PINT

GOBLET

SNIFTER

MUG

WEISS

There is, however, a unique fashionista breed of Beer Snob that has completely bought into the Belgian marketing glass scheme and places great importance on coordinating its beer with its perfect outfit, er, glass. Anybody who's spent beercentric time on any of the social media sites has surely come across the Glass Snob. You post a pic online of an incredible double IPA poured into your favorite Tripel Karmeliet tulip only to get an immediate reply from your "friend" (whom you've never actually met): "Glassware fail. At least get the right country."

Can I Get a Glass for This?

A BEER GEEK ALWAYS drinks his beer from some sort of glass, not the bottle or can it came in. While the tongue can detect general tastes such as sour, sweet, and bitter, any of the more subtle nuances, such as fruity hop notes or spicy Belgian yeast phenols, are actually being picked up by your nose. Drinking straight from a bottle or can cuts out these nuances, causing beers to come across as boring and one-dimensional. It's *always* okay to ask a server or bartender for a glass if you're not given one — just don't make a big deal about it. Advocacy, not snobbery, is the best path to spreading beery enlightenment.

KNOW YOUR BEER GLASS

While it may be fun to match the glass and its beer, most Beer Geeks would rather spend the time, space, money, and overall energy on acquiring actual beer. Instead of being a Glass Snob, a Beer Geek will simply be sure to have the standard collection of beer glasses (an assortment of tulips, snifters, and weiss glasses, mostly) and, most importantly, will know how to appropriately match them to a beer. Here is all you need to know about glass types:

TULIP. The go-to, all-purpose glass for the Beer Geek. Its bulbous base captures volatile aromatics while the tapered top displays impressive head retention. The lip is the perfect finishing touch, though, as its outward curve makes for easy drinking. This is not a sipping glass.

When to use: Any aromatic beer (IPA, saison, stout) drunk at a medium pace. Or even a high pace, for that matter.

SNIFTER. Originally designed for drinking port and sherry, the combination of a wide, swollen base and narrow opening traps the otherwise fleeting aromatics of these fortified wines. It does the same for aroma-rich beers. The base accommodates palming if the beer needs to be warmed with the hands (plus, it makes you look mighty sophisticated). The narrow mouth forces slow sipping. Head retention is poor due to high surface area of the bulbous base.

When to use: For contemplative, sipping beers where head retention is a non-issue. Mostly strong ales and vintage beers.

SHAKER (PINT). The scourge of the Beer Geek. This glass was not made with any sort of drinking purpose in mind, but rather to serve as the top to a cocktail shaker. Unfortunately, due to their durability, low cost, and stackability, the shaker has become the glass of choice for the vast majority of bars. Its near-cylindrical shape captures no aroma and provides poor head retention. A lack of stem or handle forces the drinker to warm the beer with his hands, and the thick walls make for a relatively large thermal mass, so a cold beer poured in a hot, just-from-the-dishwasher glass becomes a warm beer. Plus, the shape is about as aesthetically pleasing as a broomstick. It does, however, facilitate high-volume swilling.

When to use: Best suited for drinking water or beers that resemble water.

NONIC (ENGLISH PINT). Basically a shaker glass with a slight bulge on the upper portion. Contrary to popular belief, the bulge serves no sensory purpose and is only present to keep the lip of the glass from being chipped as well as to provide a better grip. Shares all the same shortcomings of the shaker pint.

MUG/STEIN. Same pitfalls as the shaker pint but with a distinct advantage: a handle to prevent unintentional warming of the beer. Still, really only suited for high-volume swilling (e.g., at Oktoberfest).

WHALES (ALSO KNOWN AS WALES OR WALEZ) are very rare beers. Not rare like a Bourbon County Brand Stout; rare like a Bourbon County Brand Stout Rare. (Confused? See **BCBS** and **Rare** in the Beer Geek Dictionary, page 188.) Among the glass-loving Beer Geeks, a piece of ultra-rare glassware (yes, this exists) is known as a glasswale. These glasses are often old, discontinued glasses from beloved breweries, or glasses that were distributed during a special event.

WEISS GLASS. A tall glass with a narrow bottom and wide, slightly tapering top. The volume of these glasses is oversized to accommodate the large amount of head associated with certain beers, namely German wheats. The sustained, fluffy head traps the volatile, fruity esters and other aromatics, resulting in a beautiful presentation. German bar owners learned long ago that for every weiss beer sold in a weiss glass, they'll sell 10 more to the "I-vant-vhat-they're-having" crowd.

When to use: Any pungent beer with high head production. Traditionally used for wheat beers (weisses, wits, etc.) but also superb for IPAs and other beers that have undergone dry hopping, a technique that increases head production.

GOBLET. Aesthetically pleasing and impressive, but the advantages stop there. Functionally, these glasses are the bastard offspring of an ill-conceived one-night stand between a shaker glass and a snifter with a seven-year itch. They offer nothing that a snifter or tulip has not already mastered.

When to use: Trying to impress Glass Snobs.

BEWARE!!
the Faux-Pint Glass

IF SHAKER GLASSES ARE the smelly cousin of the beer glass family, the faux-pint glass is their meth-addicted buddy. One of the vilest inventions to ever hit the beer scene, the faux-pint is a shaker glass that has been modified to contain less than a pint. These modifications typically come in the form of an extra thick bottom or a thickened lower half, though it can also come in the form of a slightly miniaturized glass. The result is a vessel that now contains 2 to 4 ounces less than the purchased "pint" of beer. Essentially outright theft when advertised as a "pint," this is the equivalent of being served a steak stuffed with sawdust. Typically found in fake Irish and English pubs, chain restaurants, airport bars, and anywhere else devoid of a regular local crowd. However, their appearance in even seemingly respectable establishments has become a disturbing trend.

REAL
PINT
(16 OZ)

FAUX
PINT
(14 OZ)

SERVING TEMPERATURE
MAXIMIZING A BEER'S PROFILE

MARKETING AGAIN AND AGAIN proclaims that beer should be served as cold as possible — even slushy, if it can be managed. This message is drilled into you from a young age, just like the message that eating double-decker burgers will help you become an Olympic athlete. But like that creepy red and yellow clown, the advertising execs are full of it.

"ICE-COLD BREWSKIS!"
"Frosty mugs!"
"THE COLDEST BEER IN TOWN!"

As a beer becomes colder, the flavors and aromas become considerably muted. The compounds that make up the aromatic qualities of a beer — fruity esters, spicy phenols, hop oils — stay hunkered down in the relative winter of an ice-cold beer. And the frosted glass only serves to numb your tongue and dull any flavors that might manage to cut a swath through the arctic environment. For the **BMC** (Bud-Miller-Coors) type of beers, this is an advantage, as considerable work has gone into making them resemble water as closely as possible, and the frigid temps further help to achieve this. After all, nobody likes a warmish glass of drinking water.

A Beer Geek is well aware that in order for a good beer to truly shine it needs to be served at its proper temperature. This will vary from style to style but generally falls within the range of 40 to 55°F. The more flavorful beers should be served on the warmer end of the spectrum and the simpler ones on the cooler side (after all, these tend to be refreshing sessionable quaffs).

By letting a beer sit out of the fridge for a short spell, a Beer Geek can achieve the perfect temperature in the comfort of his or her own home. However, when outside of the home the situation isn't always so simple. To avoid foaming issues, almost all bar and restaurant draft systems are maintained at 38°F, which greatly reduces the overall flavor profile of

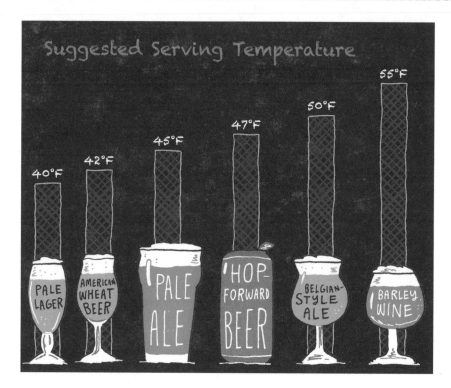

Suggested Serving Temperature

PALE LAGER	40°F
AMERICAN WHEAT BEER	42°F
PALE ALE	45°F
HOP-FORWARD BEER	47°F
BELGIAN-STYLE ALE	50°F
BARLEY WINE	55°F

most beers. If it's a truly special beer, it's entirely normal for a Beer Geek to spend a few minutes grasping the glass with both hands in an attempt warm it to a reasonable temperature. (This is done in as obvious a fashion as possible, in view of the bartender or server.)

Drinking from bottles at the bar counter, however, can sometimes present a larger temperature challenge, as the vast majority of locales keep their refrigerators at painfully low temperatures, usually at the food-sanitation mark of 35°F. At this temperature, even the finest beers will come across as one-dimensional and muted, shorting both the brewer and the drinker. This is frustrating because it typically stems from an ignorance of proper serving temps or an unwillingness to have a dedicated beer fridge.

When faced with this oft-occurring situation, a Beer Geek would do well to talk to the proprietor. Managers are often receptive to such talk, and it could lead them to rectify the issue, especially if it is a bar or restaurant that touts itself as specializing in craft beer. More passive Beer Geeks simply let their wallets do the talking and take their business elsewhere.

Damn You and Your
FROSTED MUGS

AT SOME POINT in the Beer Stone Age, it was decided that keeping thick glass mugs in the freezer was the best way to facilitate the serving of beer at a then-recommended subzero temperature — a somewhat understandable practice given the watery nature of beers at that time. Fast-forward a few decades to our era of vastly better beers, and most beer drinkers have abandoned this barbaric practice. Unfortunately, though, many bars never got the memo (cheesy chain sports bars are the likeliest offenders). For Beer Geeks already frustrated with a 38°F draft pour, this same beer served in an icy mug crosses the line. While advocacy should be the aim in nearly every situation, this is one where there's no tolerance. *A Beer Geek does not, under any circumstances, drink out of a frosted glass.* If served one, ask for a room-temperature glass in which to transfer the beer, or just send it back.

ONE-OFFS
THE ULTIMATE ATTRACTION

AS MENTIONED, BEER GEEKS LIKE to obsess about every aspect of a beer — obviously, its taste, aroma, hue, etc. — but let's face it, also its rarity.

Nothing makes a beer taste better than it being hard to come by.

It's the same mania that foodies have for the restaurant with a four-month wait list, or the car guy has for the Shelby Cobra. A Beer Geek knows it's dumb but doesn't fight it, because, well, it just feels good to get to try a beer that your buddy hasn't. IPAs that aren't distributed in-state always have a more complex hop bouquet, and a barleywine's profile is only brought to its full potential if it has a one-bottle limit.

Whether or not a brewery's beer is available in certain markets is determined by many things, most notably its distribution network but also the size of the brewery, market competition, and other factors. And there are times when even though a particular market carries a brewery's beer, a small batch size prevents the market from getting a certain release. Many of these beers are brewed only once. They are experimental batches that the brewery has no intention of adding to their regular portfolio. These are called **one-offs**.

One-offs have a special appeal for the Beer Geek. First, they're usually creative beers with weird styles or limited or expensive ingredients. Such small batches are not often cost-effective, more like a financial sacrifice made by brewers to the Beer Geeks. Second, since the plan is to make them only once, their inherent rarity makes them especially sexy.

LEGENDARY *One-offs*

DAVE
(HAIR OF THE DOG)

💧 A 29%, ice-distilled version of their famous Adam beer. Made once in 1994.

WOODEN HELL
(FLOSSMOOR STATION)

💧 In 2008, the boys at Flossmoor aged their Sheol barleywine for a year in a Woodford Reserve barrel and managed to release 360 bottles of it. They declared it never to be brewed again.

M
(MIDNIGHT SUN)

💧 A Belgian-style, barrel-aged barleywine made for the brewery's 10th anniversary. The masterwork of then head brewer and Beer Geek legend Gabe Fletcher.

LOERIK
(CANTILLON)

💧 Flemish for "lazy boy," this was a particularly delicious batch of gueuze that earned its name because it was very slow to carbonate prior to its 1998 release.

YELLOW BUS
(THE LOST ABBEY)

💧 A sour, barrel-aged wild ale aged with peaches. Helped to put The Lost Abbey firmly in Beer Geeks' headlights.

DIRTY HORSE
(DE STRUISE)

💧 A blend of 1983 and 2005 lambic, used to raise money to save a Belgian school bus route.

DON QUIJOTE
(CANTILLON)

💧 A lambic made with grapes and bottled exclusively for sale at two Italian beer bars: the Goblin Pub and the Livingstone Club.

MILLENNIUM GUEUZE
(DRIE FONTEINEN)

◊ A collaboration gueuze with De Cam, another well-respected lambic producer. Bottled in 1998 to commemorate Y2K.

MILLENNIUM
(BOSTON BEER)

◊ With only 3,000 bottles produced, this 21% bruiser released in 1999 was the predecessor of the now-cultish Utopia.

DONGS!
THE EXCLUSIVE DRAFT-ONLY, No-GROWLER BEERS

WHILE A ONE-OFF BEER IS SEXY, there is nothing that gets a Beer Geek all hot and bothered like a **DONG** (Draft Only, No Growlers). These beers are never sold by the bottle, only on draft, nor can you fill a **growler** to take home with you.

Initially it seems like a weird concept, but the approach stems from a segment of wildly popular breweries that have decided to attempt to combat the trading and reselling of their beer. This can be best explained by an example:

Russian River Brewing Company of Santa Rosa, California, makes what they call a triple IPA, Pliny the Younger. Given its cost and complexity, it is brewed only once a year. It's available solely at the brewery and to Russian River's best bar accounts across the country. When it first came out in 2005, loaded with a mindboggling amount of hops yet still surprisingly drinkable at 10.25%, Beer Geeks went crazy for it. Over the years, the hype continued to grow, and Beer Geeks began making pilgrimages to the nearest town or state that had it on tap.

The streets of Santa Rosa became overrun at release time with unruly Beer Geeks wielding crystal-sharp tulip glasses and demanding people's opinions of the Reinheitsgebot . . .

It was back in those first few years that Russian River allowed patrons to purchase growlers of Pliny the Younger at the bar. As its popularity grew, however, the crowds began to change. No longer were they made up only of Beer Geeks but also of . . . entrepreneurial folk, who started buying as many growlers as allowed. Inevitably, the next day, many of those same growlers showed up for sale on eBay at $150 a pop, to serve the market of distant Beer Geeks unable to travel to taste this über-hyped beer. Russian

River didn't take kindly to this development, for a multitude of reasons, and started banning growler fills of Pliny the Younger in 2011. Hence, the DONG was born.

To be clear, not all draft beers unavailable for growler fills are DONGs. For example, you might go to your local brewpub and find that they won't fill your growler with their barleywine, but this does not make it a DONG. For a beer to qualify, it must be in such demand that growler fills are prohibited due to resale potential, not because a brewery is trying to stop somebody from **doming** 64 ounces of 12% ABV beer.

The DONG acronym often comes up when someone new to the beer scene makes the mistake of trying to find or trade for a beer like Pliny the Younger. The online exchange usually goes something like this:

NEW GUY: *Does anyone know if any liquor stores in town carry Pliny the Younger? I love hops, and I heard this beer is very hoppy!*

BEER SNOB: *PtY is a DONG, you effin' noob.*

Handbottles

NOW, SOME FOLKS are so desperate to try a DONG that they are willing to trade for a **handbottle** of it. Handbottling refers to the practice of bringing a refillable bottle (think of a Grolsch swing top) to a bar, ordering a DONG, and then covertly emptying the glass into the bottle. Trading for handbottles is a risky proposition because it requires a lot of faith that the beer is actually what the filler says it is. Also, the quality of a beer that's been transferred multiple times is always questionable — not to mention the fact that handbottling often occurs in a bathroom stall, exponentially adding to the sketch factor. The type of people who go for such things are referred to as **tickers**, British slang for beer drinkers whose main goal is to never drink the same beer twice.

BEWARE!! THE
COLLABORATION BREW

REGIONAL DISTRIBUTION is the bane of the Beer Geek. Again, a favorite brewery will inevitably be outside of your local distribution area (the fact that this makes the beer rarer is a mere coincidence, of course). Because of this, a Beer Geek is constantly calling in favors to have friends and family ferry beers back to them whenever they travel. (You know you're a Beer Geek when people begin to change the subject after they accidentally mention their upcoming trip to Europe.)

On the surface it sounds like a great thing when a locally distributed brewery brews a collaboration beer with a favorite out-of-market brewery. For a brief time you'll have regular access to a beer that's brewed (or at least half-brewed) by the coveted out-of-market brewery. Unfortunately, though, these collaborations tend to be subpar.

The general flop of the collaboration brew can be attributed to a variety of reasons:

1. COMPROMISE

Beer is a representation of a brewer's artistic talents, paired (hopefully) with a skilled hand to execute them. However, when two of these creative minds come together, concessions have to be made to meet each of their visions, which often results in mediocrity.

2. CREATIVITY OVERDOSE

Two brewers aren't going to get together and brew the perfect pilsner. No, instead they must engage in a constant one-upmanship to show just how creative they can be. If the original idea is a saison, the end product will end up as a cactus-infused saison, steeped in Swiss iguana scrotums and aged in papier-mâché barrels that have been handcrafted by transvestite Japanese monks. In other words, a beer that tries way too hard . . . and tastes like lizard nuts.

BEER: THE ROOT OF ALL BEER GEEKERY

3. CAMARADERIE

It is a well-known fact that brewers like to drink beer with one another. When they get together there's likely going to be drinking involved. While surely fun, for obvious reasons this probably won't aid the brew process.

There have been decent collaborations, but the bottom line is, Beer Geeks do not consider a collaboration brew representative of either brewery; rather, they view it as an oddity with only a chance of being half-decent. Therefore, they reserve excitement as well as judgment.

BEER COCKTAILS
THE SCOURGE OF BEERDOM

WHILE COCKTAILS HAVE arguably been around for more than two centuries, it wasn't until Prohibition began in 1919 that they began to gain steam. Before the temperance movement cast a dark shadow over America, a lot of booze was barrel aged and artisan crafted. Rich and complex, these spirits were served neat or over ice.

But once alcohol production was moved to shady back rooms and illicit warehouses, spirits were made as quickly and cheaply as possible. Whiskey was replaced with gin because it could be made in weeks rather than years. Brand names disappeared along with quality standards. The hooch being churned out was, for the most part, harsh and foul-tasting stuff, but the thirsty public was happy to oblige a little temporary blindness in order to enjoy a drink.

To make these dreadful bathtub gins drinkable, speakeasies began to mix them with sweet syrups, fruits, and bitters to mask the off flavors, and the era of the cocktail was born. After prohibition ended, cocktails stuck and a market of legitimate "mixing" spirits emerged. Designed with simple, intense flavors to cut through the sweetness, these liquors with their harsh alcohol presence weren't a concern, as they weren't being drunk straight.

Cocktail bars are now a regular fixture in the US, and when the craft beer scene boomed, these same locales wanted in on the action. Suddenly, all of the tweed-vested, mustachioed cocktail bartenders across the country came up with the idea to blend these new popular beers with their regular array of mixers.

Pretty soon there were lambic sangrias, barleywine creamsicles, and all sorts of other beery atrocities.

What the misguided bartenders don't realize is that the beers they're mixing are masterpieces in and of themselves. They don't need additional sugars, alcohols, and fruit purees to be drinkable. A Beer Geek knows that the brewer designed and created them to stand on their own. If a beer needs all those additional ingredients, it's not worth bothering with anyway.

While this attitude *seems* to wade dangerously toward the Beer Snob category, fear not, for it couldn't be further from the truth. Beer Geeks avoid beer cocktails because the concept doesn't show respect for the care, dedication, and passion breweries put into crafting their beer. Can you picture a wine connoisseur mixing a Cotes du Rhone with Orange Crush and melon liqueur? Or a cigar aficionado smoking a grape-flavored Cohiba Robustos? A Beer Geek holds himself to the same standard.

CHAPTER 3

BREWERIES

THE EXCLUSIVE CLUB

Like anything with a dedicated following, there are certain seemingly intangible qualities that the leaders of the pack possess. These qualities often reflect a mix of the respected old guard and the boundary-pushing contemporary scene.

TAKE MUSIC, for example. Bands like the Rolling Stones have been around forever and they're well respected because they've not only created a new sound that inspired countless bands, they've also continued to innovate and remain relevant for decades. Their following is loyal, and even the most flippant music bloggers will begrudgingly give them some props.

At the same time, just about every month there is some hot new band— the new favorite of the music geeks — that is at least temporarily the greatest group ever to strum a chord. The brewing industry is no different. We've got our Stones and we have our one-hit wonders too.

FORMULA for COOL

MANY FACTORS CAN catapult a brewery to the national forefront, be it for a fleeting moment or for decades, but there is actually a method to the madness. Geeks, whether for music or for beer, want the crafters of their obsession to be geeky too. They want them to care uncompromisingly about creating the finest end product, not about making money or pleasing the masses.

Here is a list of everything a brewery needs to do right to set itself apart. Nailing one of them can get you a ticket to the demolition derby, but only the determined and crazy survive.

1. QUALITY

First and foremost, a brewery must make good beer. Or at least *some* good beer. Or, okay, one great beer.

2. STYLES

To be relevant, a brewery needs to be brewing whatever styles are popular at the time, be it aroma-forward IPAs, spontaneous sours, or barrel-aged bruisers. To have staying power, they have to be adaptable and talented enough to meet the Beer Geek's ever-changing tastes, and to do it well.

3. HOMERISM

When asked about the long-term success of Russian River Brewing Company, brewmaster Vinnie Cilurzo said, "You can't forget your locals." If they're happy, your brewery will succeed, he reasoned. Easy to say when you make some of the best hoppy and sour beers America has ever seen, but it's a valid sentiment. Beer Geeks love to talk about beer. The gossip starts with the locals and can spread like wildfire across online forums. When Beer Geeks cross paths a quick geographic pissing match often ensues, starting something like this:

BEER GEEK #1: *Where are you from?*

BEER GEEK #2: *Random City, California.*

BEER GEEK #1: *No way, I love Random City Brewing Company! Their double IPA is the best I've ever had after [insert Geek #1's hometown brewery's DIPA].*

BEER GEEK #2: *Meh, Random City used to be great, but ever since they expanded, their beers totally suck.*

Beer Geek #2's lack of homerism greatly hurt Random City's popularity, as in the next 24 hours, Beer Geek #1 will tell 302 other Beer Geeks that Random City's DIPA now tastes like garbage.

4. PARENTAGE

As mentioned, Beer Geeks want their favorite breweries to be totally committed to making the best-tasting brews, profit be damned. Because of this, a brewery's parentage is key. Who created the brewery and why? All businesses need to make money to be successful, but is there any passion behind the product, or just dollar signs? After decades of being limited to three terrible-tasting, profit-driven brands, Beer Geeks are very wary of breweries that seem too focused on the bottom line.

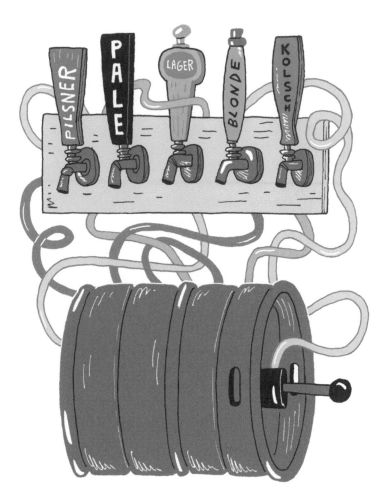

Navigating the Parentage Question

WHILE IT'S USUALLY PRETTY OBVIOUS who the Wall Street breweries are, a classic parentage issue occurs when a faux craft brewery is created by one of these conglomerates. One example is Shock Top, a Belgian-style white beer brewed by the Bud Light kings, Anheuser-Busch InBev. An alleged internal document was published by beer blogger Ben Johnson that explained how the brand's marketing strategy was to "win the battle against MicroCraft" by maintaining that their "delicious, approachable liquid" was from "a small brewer." The fact that the beer, er, "liquid," is utterly terrible, combined with their sneaky corporate tactics, makes a Beer Geek more likely to drink his own urine than a Shock Top.

There are exceptions to the conglomerate parentage rule, however, a classic example being AC Golden, a MillerCoors-owned brewery-within-a-brewery that was initially despised because of its parentage. Most Beer Geeks eventually came around on AC Golden, partly because its beers (typically fruit-steeped, barrel-aged sours) were so damn good, but also because the original brewmaster, Troy Casey (now of Casey Blending), made a concerted effort to become part of the local Beer Geek community (see *Homerism*, page 63). Beer Geeks pride themselves in always putting the quality of the beer above all else and were able to overlook AC Golden's parentage.

Another parentage situation comes up when a brewery is acquired by one of these corporate conglomerates. Again, what matters is what happens to the beer's quality. While the majority of these acquisitions have resulted in lower brewing quality due to cost-cutting measures, there are exceptions here too. A great example is Goose Island, purchased by AB InBev in 2011. The Beer Geek world bemoaned its assumed loss of the brewery's Bourbon County and Belgian-style lineup, but contrary to expectations the quality didn't drop an inch, and the production run of their specialty beers increased exponentially. While many Beer Geeks no longer buy their flagship beers (not wanting to fill the AB InBev coffers), Goose Island's specialty lineup is still moving through the Beer Geek nation as strong as ever.

5. HERITAGE

Beer Geeks are intensely devoted to the brewers who craft their favorite beers. Right or wrong, they often see a beer as the product of an individual, not a collaborative effort. Therefore, brewers can achieve celebrity status among Beer Geeks. When one of these brewers leaves to join another brewery or start their own venture, that brewery instantly has a leg up in the cool department.

The same goes for assistant brewers who worked under celebrity brewers or at star breweries. It is assumed, sometimes incorrectly, that the magical pixie dust has surely rubbed off.

6. DISTRIBUTION

Again, first and foremost, a beer must be good. But, as previously discussed, the more difficult it is to acquire, the more sought after it will be. Look no further than some of the past decade's honorees dubbed #1 Beer in the World (as determined by BeerAdvocate.com):

- *Westvleteren 12:* An absolutely delicious Belgian strong dark ale. Can be acquired only at the brewery in Belgium, and even then only with advance reservations.

- *Pliny the Younger:* The world's first triple IPA, a powerhouse of hop resin, caramel, and alcohol. Brewed only once annually and released in the month of February. Available solely on draft and at very exclusive bar accounts.

- *Heady Topper:* An intensely fruity, unfiltered double IPA. Brewed in a tiny 15-barrel brewery in Vermont and typically available only in-state at select stores.

A vast distribution is not necessarily beneficial to a beer's popularity. Nor is it always detrimental, as evidenced by well-respected breweries Stone and Sierra Nevada, but it is never helpful in earning Beer Geek adoration.

7. FLAGSHIP BEER (OR LACK THEREOF)

A good example of a flagship beer is Fat Tire by New Belgium. Beer Geeks see flagship beers as beers brewed to "keep the lights on." They will tolerate breweries that rely on a flagship beer, but just like national distribution, it is never a draw. Beer Geeks look for breweries to constantly push the envelope and evolve, which can be hard to do when a flagship is sucking resources.

Just a few years back, the thought of opening a brewery without a flagship or six-pack beer was considered unfathomable. However, the rise of craft beer has allowed breweries like Anchorage Brewing Company and The Bruery, both of which create only high-end bomber-sized brews, not only to exist but to be incredibly successful.

8. COST

It is an indisputable fact that the more expensive something is, the better it is.

Beer is no exception, and breweries that have high-priced beers are automatically known as creators of a superb product. If a brewery starts selling its beer for too cheap, they must be cutting corners and therefore not worth getting excited about.

Beer Geeks do have their pricing limit, though, as demonstrated when Against the Grain brewery began distributing. When the brewery first opened, bottles were available only locally. But after developing a cult following and seeing their beers become a hot commodity on the national beer-trading scene, they began distributing their bottles nationwide. Beer Geeks' initial excitement quickly turned to disgust when bottles of Against the Grain IPA started retailing for upwards of $18. While barrel aging or special ingredients may justify a high price tag, it's a hard thing to understand for a normal IPA. The brewery's cool factor took a very big hit, and it's taken subsequent (substantial) repricing to bring them back into Beer Geeks' good graces.

9. NOT TRYING TOO HARD

Pretty self-explanatory. Baby, be cool.

10. QUANTITY OF OFFERINGS

Beer Geeks love it when a brewery gives them choices and variations. This is viewed as dedication to the craft and a showcase of a brewery's creativity. However, a threshold exists beyond which too many beers can be a detriment to a brewery's coolness. As previously noted, Beer Geeks love to talk shop about a brewery, and it's important to stay in the know about new beers arriving on the scene. God forbid someone asks what you think about the barrel-aged version of Wee Black Mamba and you're thinking, *What in the world is Wee Black Mamba??*

For the most part, a brewery can only maintain a handful of beers in the forefront of the national Beer Geek consciousness. A Beer Geek's memory is only so-so, and she has only so much time, so many dollars, and so much liver capacity. Some breweries (*ahem*, Jester King, Bruery) are churning out different beers so fast that Beer Geeks can't keep up with them, which is not a good thing.

11. SCANT ADVERTISING

Advertising is for the masses, not the connoisseurs. Years of bitter-beer-face commercials have led Beer Geeks to believe that the quality of a beer is inversely proportional to the amount of dollars spent promoting it. Beer Geeks make it their responsibility to know everything there is to know about a beer through their own research and a collective knowledge base. Therefore, advertising is an unnecessary waste of money that could have instead been spent on crafting a better beer.

In addition, it's generally thought that the simpler the packaging and labels, the better the beer. Anybody who disagrees should look no further than Russian River's continued success despite their insistent use of the **Comic Sans** font.

12. AWARDS

Though by no means a guarantee, winning certain awards can help catapult a brewery onto the national scene. Typically, the only awards that matter are medals from the Great American Beer Festival or the World Beer Cup, while awards like the East Kansas Brewers Cup don't mean much. However, winning a GABF or WBC medal does not necessarily mean the world, either. The medal needs to be in a category that is currently captivating the Beer Geek mindset. Gold for an IPA, for example, is a huge deal. This is what pushed Societe — a previously unknown brewery, now with a cultish following — to the national forefront. On the other hand, if Joe's Bucktooth Brewery in Bumblebrook, Missouri, wins the gold in the Roggenbier category, they don't need to worry about securing the doors from the hoards of Beer Geeks.

Trade Bait?

"TRADE BAIT" IS A BEER that is universally sought after by Beer Geeks but is relatively easy to acquire by those in the beer's local area. The locals can use this beer to trade with non-local Beer Geeks for just about any other beer they could ever want. A few classic examples are Heady Topper in Vermont, Casey Brewing and Blending in Colorado, de Garde in Oregon, and Toppling Goliath in Iowa. Every Beer Geek who trades wants to live in an area that has some sort of trade bait.

THE BEER GEEK FORMULA

Fill out the survey below to determine if that unknown brewery has what it takes to make it to national-level Beer Geek fandom:

1. Quality of the beer?

a. Epic ....50 POINTS

b. Good .... 10 POINTS

c. Okay .... 0 POINTS

d. Bad .... -50 POINTS

Points ....

2. How relevant are the beers produced in terms of current trends?

a. Spot-on .... 20 POINTS

b. Here and there.....15 POINTS

a. One relevant, and a whole bunch of fruited honey blondes ..10 POINTS

d. WASP menu (Wheat, Amber, Stout, Pale)...... -25 POINTS

Points ....

3. Do they distribute?

a. Yes .... 10 POINTS

b. No .... 0 POINTS

Points ....

4. How many states do they distribute to?

a. 1–2.............. 10 POINTS

b. 3–5 .... 2 POINTS

c. 6 or more .... 0 POINTS

Points ....

5. How many people attend a brewery event (release, tapping, etc.)?

a. 100+ .... 10 POINTS

b. 50–99............. 5 POINTS

c. Fewer than 50 .....0 POINTS

Points ....

6. Are they owned by an outside source?

a. No................ 0 POINTS

b. Yes .... -25 POINTS

Points ....

7. Did the head brewer formerly work in a Top 250 brewery?

a. Yes . . . . 10 POINTS

b. No . . . . 0 POINTS

Points . . . . [ ]

8. Do they sell six packs?

a. No . . . . 10 POINTS

b. Yes . . . . 0 POINTS

Points . . . . [ ]

9. Do they sell bombers?

a. Yes . . . . 10 POINTS

b. No . . . . -10 POINTS

Points . . . . [ ]

10. Cost of the bomber?

a. Over $25 . . . . .5 POINTS

b. $15–$24 . . . . .10 POINTS

c. $10–14. . . . . .5 POINTS

d. Less than $10 . . . . . .0 POINTS

Points . . . . [ ]

11. Have they won GABF or WBC awards?

a. Yes, and for a trendy style . . . . . . 10 POINTS

b. Yes, but for an unexciting style . . . . . 1 POINT

c. No . . . . 0 POINTS

Total points . . . . [ ]

♦ **110–150**: *Chances are, you're already behind the curve and Beer Geeks know all about this brewery.*

♦ **100–109**: *Trade bait! Be the best homer you can be and start hyping up that brewery!*

♦ **80–99**: *There's definitely some potential here. Start dropping some hints to the brewers about styles or distribution.*

♦ **60–79**: *Not a bad joint, but doesn't have what it takes to cut it in the big show.*

♦ **59 OR FEWER**: *Bumsville. Too many good breweries out there to waste your time on this one.*

. . . .

TOTAL POINTS

THE CLASSICS
PIONEERS OF THE GEEK FRONTIER

LET'S CONTINUE WITH the music industry analogy: Which breweries are going to be the ones that make it to the classic rock and oldies stations? Who are the Beatles and the Rolling Stones of the beer world? As with music, these breweries have to be popular and groundbreaking when they first hit the scene but also have the staying power to remain applicable today.

The following is a list (in no particular order) of those breweries — the golden oldies, if you will — that have long been revered and respected by Beer Geeks:

SIERRA NEVADA BREWING COMPANY. Sierra Nevada made hoppy beers way before it was cool, or even really a thing. In fact, they made it okay to be audacious with hops. The Sierra Nevada Pale Ale (SNPA) forever changed the face of the American beer scene and blazed the path for hop lovers. Released in 1981, SNPA was unlike anything else out there. Bursting with in-your-face, we-don't-care-if-you-like-it hoppiness, it was quintessentially American. And while they could have sat back and rested on their laurels, they instead continue to push the envelope with new, fantastic, boundary-shoving beers.

BOSTON BEER COMPANY. *Whoa*, many will say. *Sam Adams? The archetypal, there-is-nothing-else-but-shitty-BMC-beers-on-tap-so-I-guess-I'll-drink-it beer?* Yes, those guys. While now relegated to airport bar consumption, their most popular beer led the charge against the flavorless, watered-down beer scene of the '80s. Boston Beer and a handful of others fought the David vs. Goliath battle to share tap space among the BMCs in many bars, and for that Beer Geeks owe them a debt of gratitude. They make this list because, while not with stunning fashion, they do continue to create occasionally progressive beers in their Brewmaster's Collection and have a handful of cult-worthy offerings like Utopia and Millennium.

BELL'S BREWERY. Any Beer Geek knows that Michigan is a helluva beer state. Of course, where there is snow and dark, there will be lots of beer, but it is because of Bell's that Michigan is the beer mecca it is today. Their incredible attention to detail when crafting immensely drinkable, balanced beers won over the swill drinkers of the Wolverine state. While Bell's is not necessarily known for putting out new beers, the same ones that put them on the map, like Two Hearted Ale, Expedition Stout, and Hopslam, continue to be beloved by Beer Geeks today.

BROOKLYN BREWERY. The East Coast beer scene was a tough horse to break in. Stubborn and loyal, the beer drinkers along the Atlantic seaboard weren't too interested in new, fancypants beer. Brooklyn helped break down those walls, particularly with their incredibly approachable Brooklyn Lager. And by offering more aggressive beers like Black Chocolate Stout and Sorachi Ace, they've been able to maintain a seat at the cool kids' table.

AUTHENTIC LAMBIC BLENDERS. The various lambic brewers and blenders in the Senne Valley (Cantillon, Drie Fonteinen, Girardin, Hanssens, etc.) are about as cool as it gets right now. Just a decade or so ago, these guys were on the brink of extinction, their own countrymen abandoning this offbeat style in favor of more "approachable" beers. But then, wandering Beer Geeks discovered and fell in love with this funky, tart beer style and have since slowly built them up to godlike stature.

RUSSIAN RIVER BREWING COMPANY. After breweries like Bell's and Sierra Nevada forged a path for good beer in America, a new guard of breweries popped up in the early 2000s and pushed the scene even further. Russian River took hoppiness to a whole new level with beers like Pliny the Elder and Pliny the Younger and then really blew the roof off the scene with funky, sour, barrel-aged beers like Consecration and Beatification. Even a decade later their beers are the high-water marks that most in these styles are judged against.

THE LOST ABBEY. The Lost Abbey was created to allow then Pizza Port brewmaster Tomme Arthur a chance to play in his Belgian beer sandbox. Before The Lost Abbey, the thought of an American brewery making only high-end specialty Belgian-style beers and selling them in corked 750-mL bottles for $10 or more was considered financial suicide. Arthur's beer proved them wrong and helped give birth to the beer bomber scene we enjoy today.

ALLAGASH BREWING COMPANY. While Belgian-style beers are made everywhere in America today, this was definitely not the case in the mid '90s. Allagash founder Rob Tod decided to do something about that in 1995 and released White, a wit-style beer that most agree can go toe-to-toe with any of the Belgian classics. The rest is history, and Allagash continues to make really awesome, really expensive Belgian-style beers in small enough batches (mmmm, rarity) to keep Beer Geeks drooling and happy.

GOOSE ISLAND BEER COMPANY. Starting as brewpub in 1988, Goose Island made then-progressive beers, like ambers, hefeweizens, and IPAs, and managed to make a bit of a name for itself. The beer world continued to turn, though, and breweries like GI became a dime a dozen. Seemingly destined to be forgotten, GI was instead forever enshrined in the Beer Geek Hall of Fame when it released its 14% ABV Bourbon County Brand Stout (BCBS) in 2003. This beer changed the barrel-aged strong beer scene. Just like Sierra Nevada Pale Ale did with hops, BCBS brought an American attitude to oak and alcohol, and Beer Geeks absolutely adored it. Not quite satisfied yet, GI began releasing variants of the beer made with additional ingredients (coffee, vanilla, coconut, blackberries) or aged in different types of spirit barrels. These small batches of variants fed the Beer Geek fever and helped spawn a movement of one-off batch variations of classic beers from breweries across the country. When Goose Island was purchased in 2011 by AB InBev (the multinational alcohol corporation best known for stepping on the throats of craft brewers everywhere), Beer Geek Nation assumed the worst.

Instead, the moneymen at AB InBev realized that not only were Beer Geeks not going anywhere, their money didn't actually smell too bad.

The amount of BCBS increased, the number of variants doubled, and Beer Geeks responded with an ever-growing frenzy for this delicious bruisin' ale, proving that it's ultimately about what's in the bottle.

JOLLY PUMPKIN ARTISAN ALES. Along with Lost Abbey, Jolly Pumpkin is definitely the youngest of the "pioneers" to make this list. And just like Lost Abbey, the brewery is known for being a trailblazer in the I'm-only-going-to-make-the-kind-of-beer-I-want-and-sell-it-in-bombers scene.

But, while Lost Abbey was making Belgian-inspired ales, Jolly Pumpkin was making beers that nobody had ever dreamed of — beers that fit no style category but were damn delicious.

The average person didn't know what to make of this, but Beer Geeks felt like they finally had a guide.

DESCHUTES BREWERY. Opened in 1988, Deschutes will always remain beloved for being part of the original group of trailblazers responsible for the beery choices we experience today. Even though it resides in the midst of Pacific Northwest hop country, it became best known for its unhoppy Black Butte Porter, which opened beer drinkers' minds to the idea that a roasted beer could be sessionable too. They truly gained the Beer Geeks' admiration, though, when they began releasing ultra-progressive, ultra-limited, barrel-aged vintage beers like Abyss and Dissident.

HAIR OF THE DOG BREWING COMPANY. In 1993, when Alan Sprints opened Hair of the Dog with the sole offering of a smoky, 10% ABV German barley-wine, set to retail in single 12-oz. bottles for a then-outrageous $5, people told him he was nuts. Now, more than 20 years later, it's become apparent how wrong those people were.

STONE BREWING COMPANY. The brewery originally made a name for itself in 1997 with its oh-so-cleverly named Arrogant Bastard Ale. In the '90s, the beer's moniker seemed to strike a chord with bar and restaurant owners wanting to appear hip. This, paired with the fact that the beer was damn good, made Stone a nationwide success. Founder Greg Koch has a dangerous combination of kookiness, creativity, and business savvy that has kept the brewery on the leading edge of beery trends.

AVERY BREWING COMPANY. Another '90s-era trailblazer that helped the Rocky Mountain region gain its well-earned reputation as a craft beer destination. While its six-pack offerings don't elicit as much excitement from Beer Geek Nation nowadays, its massive dedication to making extremely small-batch, high-ABV, barrel-aged beers has recaptured the fervor of beer traders worldwide and made Avery relevant once again.

DOGFISH HEAD. With a penchant for creative flair, founder Sam Calagione is probably the most recognizable craft beer celebrity in the world, starring in the *Brew Wars* movie as well as his own TV show, *Brew Masters*. While Dogfish Head has never made boring, run-of-the mill beers, it has made its name by continually pushing the boundaries of what is considered beer. Some feel this puts it more often on the bleeding edge rather than the cutting edge, resulting in a very tumultuous relationship with many Beer Geeks. Regardless, most Beer Geeks know of Dogfish Head's indelible impact on the craft beer movement and give it its due.

NEW BELGIUM BREWING COMPANY. Along with its East Coast brethren Allagash, New Belgium was created by beer lovers tired of being unable to enjoy their favorite Belgian beer in America. Through the '90s and early 2000s, it helped educate Americans on all the delicious styles of beer we'd been missing out on. The release of its tart Flanders red ale, La Folie, in 2001 helped spark the sour beer revolution, which has led to a new generation of sour beer lovers in America.

HAS-BEENS, SELLOUTS,
AND OTHER GARBAGE

THERE ARE NOT TOO MANY hated breweries in the Beer Geek world. For the most part, Beer Geeks reserve their disdain for the BMC conglomerates, the band of evil super-businessmen out to rid the world of good beer through DC lobbying, legal strong-arming, and shady distribution tactics. They're giant for a reason, and the rise of craft beer has not gone unnoticed by them, as evidenced by the rise of their faux craft breweries. You've certainly seen these beers — made by the big boys, but marketed and sold under the guise of a small independent craft brewery — but you may not have realized it.

The most notable of the faux crafters are probably Shock Top and Blue Moon, though how these beers/breweries are viewed by Beer Geeks is interesting. To say that Blue Moon is beloved by Beer Geeks would not be true, but most will begrudgingly give it props as a decent Belgian-style wit. After all, it's not like the BMC guys are bad brewers — in fact, this couldn't be further from the truth. It's just that rather than aiming to craft the most flavorful, enjoyable beer, their criteria are often based on creating flavorless, low-cost lagers that can be consumed in large volumes. And they do it exceptionally well. When they want to apply their talents, beers like Blue Moon can happen. Shock Top, however, is at the other end of the spectrum. Sugary sweet and tasting of sickly artificial flavoring, it drinks more like a Belgian wit–inspired soda pop. Again, it's all about the beer.

Besides those from the low end of the faux breweries, the other looked-down-upon beers are those from foreign macrobreweries. Back in the '80s and '90s, the American beer scene was dominated by the BMCs, and imported beers like Bass, Guinness, and Fosters were relished as flavorful exotics. And compared to a Miller Lite, it was certainly true.

However, in this current era of craft beer bliss, these beers now come across as being as bland and stale as day-old Cream of Wheat.

The last category that draws the ire of the Beer Geeks is the has-been crowd. These are the once-great breweries that, at some point, sold out to the giant global beer conglomerates. The purchasing companies are all about the bottom line and drive their newly acquired breweries to gradually make their beer more "palatable" to the masses by stripping out anything that resembles character and flavor.

Your Brewery is, uh, NO GOOD!

GUINNESS

Ahh, the black Irish gold. Guinness is often a person's gateway beer into Beer Geekdom, and for that we owe it a special thanks. But as a palate progresses, the realization slowly dawns that there isn't much to this beer beyond the roasted malt bite. And then there are the infamous "Guinness farts," a phenomenon perhaps due to the ridiculous amount of additives used in making the beer. This unfortunate gastrointestinal distress has led many nonconverts to believe that all flavorful beers make you stink up a room.

STELLA ARTOIS

Belgian beer has a very impressive reputation. And Stella Artois is easily the highest selling Belgian-brewed beer in the United States. For that reason, it's easy for many to assume that this bland, insipid lager is representative of the Belgian beer scene. This is an unfortunate and incorrect conclusion. Examining its fancy, gold-foil-rimmed packaging, a wise man once remarked, "You can put a pig in a tuxedo, but this beer still tastes like shit."

LEINENKUGEL

Leinenkugel is an old-school Wisconsin brewery that was bought out by MillerCoors (or whatever they're called now) in 2011. Two words: Summer Shandy. Barf.

CULT BREWERIES
THE PINNACLES OF THE BREWING WORLD

WITHIN THE GROUP OF BREWERIES that get Beer Geeks in a frenzy there is the constantly rotating upper echelon, an elite class of the world's hottest breweries. The buzz around these outfits goes far beyond your average joint with a loyal following. Rather, they command a cultish devotion among Beer Geeks: pilgrimages are made to visit the sacred grounds, brewing logos are tattooed on bodies, and rare white whales are preserved in cellars as relics to be viewed but never drunk.

To get a pass into this exclusive club, breweries must not only meet the prereqs of the Formula for Cool (see page 62), they must do at least two of them — and usually more — exceptionally well. If you make a world-class IPA and happen to be in the middle of nowhere, you'll manage to garner a few fans. But treat your locals right to build up that homerism angle and you could have a brewery that Beer Geeks will plan their vacations around.

In addition, cult breweries almost always have some sort of intangible element that contributes to their rabid following. It's an elusive thing, and varies from brewery to brewery. Crooked Stave's comes from creator Chad Yakobson's groundbreaking master's thesis on *Brettanomyces*, while Hill Farmstead's rises from their (somewhat uncomfortable) obsession with naming beers after obscure philosophical arguments. But all cult breweries have that something special that seems to separate them from the pack.

The last thing that they all seem to have in common is that they're relatively new to the scene. With few exceptions (such as Cantillon and Russian River), once a brewery bursts on the scene Beer Geeks develop an intense, devoted following . . . until the next big thing comes along. Cult breweries aren't immune to the fickleness of Beer Geeks.

While the secret to attaining cult status may seem a bit muddy, the most important aspects are actually very simple. A brewery needs to do only two things:

1. Brew at least one beer that's considered a whale, and 2. Be a destination-worthy brewery.

If it doesn't meet both of these criteria, it doesn't count. For example, Boston Beer has Millennium, a beer considered by any standard to be a whale. However, Boston Beer is not going to be the focal point of any Beer Geek's beercation, and is thus not a cult brewery.

While this may seem an appropriate place to include a list of cult breweries, such a list would be out of date by the time you finish reading this chapter. Instead, any burgeoning Beer Geek looking to get the current cult breweries on her radar would be best served by checking out the breweries whose beers are on the *Top 250 Beers* list on BeerAdvocate.com, which is constantly updated and is based on user reviews. While there are certainly a handful of breweries on their list that don't really have a cult following (Brasserie de Rochefort, for example), the vast majority do, making it a great barometer of Beer Geeks' latest loves.

ARE YOU A FANBOY/GIRL?

While it's great to like and respect a specific brewery, a Beer Geek always takes care to ensure he/she doesn't venture into the fanboy/girl realm of loyalty. Folks in this category unequivocally love every beer that their chosen brewery makes (regardless of the quality), and in turn bash everything that competing breweries release. There definitely are amazing breweries out there, but every single one of them has turned out a turd at least once. Even Alpine Beer Company, the great San Diego brewery with an entire legion of fanboys, has their Willy Wheat.

Check "yes" or "no" (and let's be honest, now):

YES   **NO**   *Have you ever . . .*

☐   ☐   **1.** concurrently worn two articles of clothing bearing the name of the same brewery?

☐   ☐   **2.** claimed to have "loved" a beer from a brewery, even though you've never actually had it?

☐   ☐   **3.** defensively called someone else a fanboy/girl?

☐   ☐   **4.** made analogies involving Zelda or Final Fantasy when talking about beer?

☐   ☐   **5.** . . . claimed that one brewery is "totally ripping off" another brewery's beer or branding?

If you answered "yes" to more than one of the above, you're teetering dangerously close to the fanboy/girl line.

THE BEER GEEK
HALL OF FAME

BEHIND EVERY GREAT pioneering brewery is a personality — sometimes the brewer, sometimes not — that helped launch the operation into Beer Geek stardom. It's for these individuals that the Beer Geek Hall of Fame was created.

Entrance to the Beer Geek Hall of Fame is an honor bestowed only on those select few who have helped to both create and inspire the Beer Geek lifestyle. These individuals have elevated beer from merely the sticky substance that coated fraternity floors (or at least one of the substances) to the sophisticated craft beverage it is today. Their contributions have made them Beer Geek household names.

TOMME ARTHUR

*Co-founder and director
of brewery operations at
The Lost Abbey*

Tomme Arthur is known
primarily for bringing Belgian-
style beers to the forefront of
American beer culture with his
brewery The Lost Abbey. He is
also the creator of such white
whales as Yellow Bus and Duck
Duck Gooze. Though his serious
nature (think John Wayne stare-
down) can been misinterpreted,
he's proven to be nothing but
gracious to his legions of fans, and
his role in helping create the all-
important San Diego beer scene
will forever enshrine him in the
Hall of Fame.

VINCENT CILURZO

*Co-owner and brewmaster at
Russian River Brewing*

The Golden Boy of the Beer Geek scene,
"Vinnie," as he is affectionately known,
can do no wrong. His résumé of both
sour and hoppy beers, which includes
numerous whales (Beatification, Pliny
the Younger), is unmatched in the mod-
ern Beer Geek era. His generosity in
sharing knowledge with both brewers
and beer drinkers alike has helped cul-
tivate the spirit of brotherhood found in
the craft beer industry today.

VAN ROY FAMILY
Lambic brewers/blenders at Brasserie Cantillon

Without the vigilance of the Van Roy family over the past century, there is a good chance the world would have lost the lambic beers that Beer Geeks drool over today. Jean-Pierre Van Roy made a name for Cantillon by making unapologetically dry and tart beers with a variety of creative ingredients. Now son-in-law Jean carries the torch and, with it, a particular aptitude for knowing just what Beer Geeks want . . . before they know it themselves.

GREG KOCH
Co-founder and CEO of Stone Brewing

Having the audacity to name a beer Arrogant Bastard — and have it actually be good — was critical in setting the tone and expectations for the '90s craft beer boom. By continually managing to remain relevant (despite a rather trying love affair with seemingly endless three-way collaborations), Koch has elevated himself to Beer Geek stardom. No relation to Jim.

GARRETT OLIVER
Brewmaster at Brooklyn Brewery

Never has the beer world seen a man so media savvy as Garrett Oliver. When your co-worker excitedly tells you that she saw a guy on TV talking about how beer is made and how it pairs with food, there's a 99 percent chance it's him. No one has done more to bring craft beer to the forefront of American culture.

SAM CALAGIONE
Founder and president of Dogfish Head Brewing

He's the brewmaster who has shaken more hands than a presidential candidate. You're not really a Beer Geek until you've had your picture taken with Sam at some beer festival, tap takeover, or other event. The man seems to be in a million places at once, but Dogfish Head still manages to crank out quality, boundary-pushing beers on a regular basis. Though he almost lost admittance to the hall with the release of Chicha (a beer made with maize and brewers' saliva), with a few flashes of his dazzling whites all was forgiven.

MICHAEL JACKSON
Beer writer extraordinaire

When a Beer Geek hears the name Michael Jackson, his thoughts don't turn to a one-gloved singer but rather to an eloquent, wild-haired English writer. Known as the Beer Hunter, Jackson began scouring the globe in the 1970s in search of then-obscure beers. His tireless travels resulted in the legendary books *The World Guide to Beer* (1977) and *The Great Beers of Belgium* (1991), both of which forever changed the way we view beer.

ARMAND DEBELDER
Lambic brewer/blender at Drie Fonteinen

A second-generation lambic blender, Armand, like Jean-Pierre Van Roy, fought valiantly to ensure that Beer Geeks of today can enjoy authentic gueuze. Famously refusing to sell an entire year's worth of lambic because he deemed it subpar due to a heater malfunction in the cellar, he forever captured a place in all Beer Geeks' hearts.

KEN GROSSMAN
Founder and CEO of Sierra Nevada Brewing Company

Who knows what the beer world would be like if it weren't for Ken Grossman's iconic Sierra Nevada Pale Ale. This first mainstream craft beer was a showcase of American hops and built the foundation for the Headys and Nelsons that we relish today.

JIM KOCH
Co-founder and chairman of Boston Beer

By creating Samuel Adams Boston Lager, Koch (Beer Geeks know it's pronounced "cook" and don't awkwardly mumble "cock") waged the war to bring craft beer to the masses and now satisfies the thirst of thousands stuck in airports during long layovers.

THE ALSTRÖM BROTHERS
Founders of BeerAdvocate.com

Commonly known as "the Bros," Jason and Todd Alström created the website BeerAdvocate.com in 1996 as a "global, grassroots network, powered by an independent community of beer enthusiasts and industry professionals who are dedicated to supporting and promoting beer." Anybody who has searched the web for beer info has surely come across this website. The internet has heaped fuel onto the raging bonfire that is the world of craft beer, and the Bros have been instrumental in directing and focusing that fuel. Though some may grumble that they moderate their website with an iron fist, all can agree that the craft beer scene would not be where it is today if the Bros had instead decided to create CheeseAdvocate.com.

STAYING CURRENT
INTERNET FORUMS

No Beer Geek lives on an island. In this rapidly trending world of craft beer, staying up to date requires constant monitoring. While information can come from blogs, friends, social media, and the like, the bulk of information seems to be disseminated through a few online beer discussion websites, most notably RateBeer.com and BeerAdvocate.com. In fact, most will admit that our current beer renaissance can be credited, in part, to them.

Before Al Gore turned the final screw on his magical World Wide Web machine, many beer lovers were left stranded in BMC-swilling parts of the world with no like-minded individuals with whom to share their beers, ideas, and frustrated tears.

Now, thanks to these websites, we have a flourishing global Beer Geek network.

The focus of both sites is about evenly split between user-supplied beer reviews and a hodgepodge of various discussion threads. However, the two sites have decidedly different tones that attract different types of Beer Geeks.

BEERADVOCATE (BA) was founded by two brothers, Jason and Todd Alström, and is operated out of Massachusetts. They're known to rule their site with an iron first. The motto is "Respect Beer," and everything on BA is about beer. Off-topic posts, trolling, inflammatory reviews, etc., are deleted immediately, and they have no problem canceling the accounts of repeat offenders. Posting memes will get you a digital hand-smack. People with an anything-goes attitude regarding the internet are apt to get up in arms about this policing. However, BA is a treasure trove of information, and there is no better place to connect with regional beer lovers. Plus, a tyrannical rule helps keep some of the snobs in check.

RATEBEER, based out of Sonoma, is a more relaxed forum. "Macho Man" Randy Savage GIFs float through discussion threads, and Beer Geeks are free to talk sports trash on random posts. Beer reviews are typically very short (fewer than 50 words), with simple descriptors rather than sentences (BA beer reviews are usually in essay form and contain all sorts of flowery language). RateBeer seems to attract a much larger international community, probably due to the less intimidating, more laissez-faire approach. This can be a boon to Beer Geeks looking to make some transcontinental connections.

Regardless of the website you choose, it is absolutely essential to follow at least one of them to stay up to date on beer releases, trends, and happenings. The beer world is ever-changing, and it takes constant vigilance to stay on top of current events. After all, part of being a Beer Geek is knowing all about everything going on in the world of beer.

Cards to the Chest

IN GENERAL, internet forums are friendly and relatively welcoming to newcomers. However, the classic noob mistake is to give away too much information.

Every city has a handful of stores that are considered "hidden gems": because they are small and out-of-the-way, these places have a better chance of retaining limited-release beers. Mentioning these shops online is a surefire way to earn the wrath of the local online beer community. Same goes for when a bar taps a keg of ultra-rare beer, or a shipment of a whale-ish beer hits town. Beer Geeks put a lot of liverwork into finding and even cultivating these spots and are none too happy when all of a sudden the whole world knows about them. Once that info is out, it stays out.

Additionally, asking for this information in the classic "What stores got the [insert latest beer release] in?" thread is generally considered poor form and lazy. Beer Geeks are expected to form a group of local contacts (a phone tree of sorts), through which this information is usually disseminated.

CHAPTER 4
PROCUREMENT:
THE BEER
AND OTHER GEEKY GOODS

While it starts to seem that being a Beer Geek is all about information gathering, at some point actual beer has to be acquired and consumed. And in reality, this is (at least it should be) what really gets a Beer Geek out of bed in the morning (or perhaps what keeps one in bed . . .).

BEER GEEKS RELISH the hunt and chase to find those elusive beers they've heard so much about. And when hunting, Beer Geeks follow a whole set of strategies and guidelines that they've communally gathered over the years, helping them become ultra-efficient in capturing their prey.

LIQUOR STORES AND
THEIR BEER GUYS:
TYPES AND STRENGTHS

WITH ALL THE LIMITED-RELEASE BEERS to chase and vintage bottles to find, no Beer Geek should rely on just one liquor store. Different stores have different strengths, and it's important that a Beer Geek maintain a bevy of harpoons when out hunting for whales.

First and foremost, every Beer Geek needs to have a small mom-and-pop shop that no one knows about. This is where to head when that hyped beer has been bought out everywhere else in town. Another essential is the mega-warehouse. Even though 90 percent of their airplane hangar of a building is used to store Coors Light, some definite bargains can be had here. Don't get overwhelmed by their massive selection; instead take just a few minutes to peruse their craft beer section. And, finally, you can't forget the high-end wine-store-turned-craft-beer-headquarters. It's this locale where you can encounter some very obscure beers, albeit at a premium (unfortunately, Master Cicerone–certified clerks don't come cheap).

Next, it's absolutely essential that at each of these locales the Beer Geek befriends the Beer Guy. While the duties of this fine individual vary from place to place, some sort of beer guy exists in every single store. In the small shop, they'll likely stock the beer, sweep the floors, and even ring you up. In the warehouse, this fellow will spend most of his time in an office combing through paperwork and organizing store events. Regardless, his crucial duty, the one that earns him the esteemed "beer guy" title, is choosing exactly which beer to order.

It is for this sole reason that the beer guy must be befriended, because after all, he holds the key to the elusive beery castle.

Want to know when that one-off double IPA is coming to town? The beer guy knows. Going to be on vacation when the latest Toppling Goliath beer is released? The beer guy can hold one for you. Curious to know if any of that shipment of vintage gueuze is still around? The beer guy may just be able to rustle up a bottle from the shadows. Not sure if it's a freckle or melanoma? The beer guy's cousin is the best dermatologist in town.

Disclaimer

THE TERM "BEER GUY" is inherently sexist. However, for whatever reason, the vast, vast majority of store employees who place beer orders have penises. It is unclear why this is so, but it may have to do with the fact that the bulk of their day is spent hefting kegs around, lurking in 35-degree walk-in coolers, and talking to insufferable Beer Snobs — all of which perhaps most of the females of the species have been smart enough to avoid. But regardless of the tradesperson's gender, the term "beer guy" just seems right.

However, before you go buying them boxes of chocolates, be aware that not all beer guys are as solid as the next. Just because they happen to hold this position of power does not excuse them from needing to earn a Beer Geek's devotion. So how do you determine if your beer guy is up to snuff? A good one should know everything about the local beer distribution scene, including:

◊ *Anything and everything about every beer offering on the shelves*

◊ *New breweries arriving on the scene*

◊ *What the upcoming limited releases are*

◊ *How many cases of each offering are coming in*

◊ *How quickly a particular beer will sell*

Unfortunately, it's an incredible rarity to find a beer guy possessing all of these traits. Though craft beer is taking over a bigger and bigger slice of the pie, most beer guys' attention often is dominated by the BMC scene. BMC still reigns as the largest (by volume) chunk of their beer selection (and sales), after all. Therefore, it is often up to the Beer Geek to mold his beer guy into an ideal form. Through a process much like training a dog, simple tasks can be ingrained via direct, positive reinforcement.

BEER GUY TRAINING GUIDELINES

To mold the perfect beer guy (article coming soon to a *Cosmopolitan* near you), a Beer Geek first needs to know what he's working with. Here are the three general beer guy types:

CLUELESS JOE

HABITAT: Strip mall liquor stores

LIKES: Jack Link's Beef Nuggets, Mountain Dew

STRENGTHS: Store has lack of competition from other Beer Geeks

THINGS TO WATCH OUT FOR: Lack of craft beer knowledge; store has poor overall selection

TRAINING TIPS: Ask him to order limited-release beers and reward him by regularly buying them

This guy has worked his way up the ranks in the store. Starting off as a shelf stocker, he's proved his worth by showing up to work most days, and relatively sober at that. Therefore he's been awarded the task of beer ordering. Joe's furthest venture into craft beer has been Bud Light Lime, but he understands there's a market for fancypants beer, regardless of how weird it tastes. Joe won't understand your obsession, but he can help fill your geekish needs if he's around and it's not too much work.

WINE SNOB
JACQUES

HABITAT: Wine-centric stores

LIKES: Vintage Bordeaux, turtlenecks

STRENGTHS: Store carries high-end beers

THINGS TO WATCH OUT FOR: Expensive beers, craft beer ignorance

TRAINING TIPS: Tolerate misguided advice

Jacques works in a wine shop that happens to sell beer. He can readily tell you the terroir difference between a Côte de Nuits and a Ladoix Grand Cru, so knowing all there is to know about beer is a piece of cake. There are really only one or two types anyway, right? Since beer is so simple, he finds it best to use vague adjectives like *rich*, *flavorful*, and *smooth* to describe just about any of them. *Hoppy* is another good one if the letters *I*, *P*, and *A* appear in sequence on the label. However, with the store's buying power behind him, Jacques can typically get most any beer you want. But be sure to use your best judgment when his own beer recommendations come into play.

JOHN
THE BEER GEEK

HABITAT: Beer-first bottle shops

LIKES: Whales, ultra-fresh IPAs, RateBeer.com

STRENGTHS: Store offers best beer selection in town

THINGS TO WATCH OUT FOR: Overspending on inventory

TRAINING TIPS: Buy his suggestions to help secure future whale allocations

On paper, John is the greatest thing since New Zealand hops. This guy knows everything about every beer they stock. He's up on when all the releases are coming in and is even super eager to hold beers for you. Unfortunately, every time you come to the store, John's held five additional beers that he *just knows* you'll love. All of a sudden that trip to pick up a six-pack has turned into a $75 affair made up of beer you never intended to buy. Visit John only when you need that really special beer. Or, if you're rich.

Now you're in the home stretch.

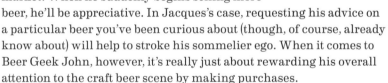

Once the beer guy types have been determined, it's relatively easy to find the best way to win them over.

It's all about gentle guidance and working around their flaws to produce results.

Positive reinforcement comes mostly in the form of purchases but can also come from taking their recommendations or turning them on to things that will help their business. With Clueless Joe, for example, you'll want to subtly refer him to a new beer on the market. When he suddenly begins selling more beer, he'll be appreciative. In Jacques's case, requesting his advice on a particular beer you've been curious about (though, of course, already know about) will help to stroke his sommelier ego. When it comes to Beer Geek John, however, it's really just about rewarding his overall attention to the craft beer scene by making purchases.

STRAIGHT FROM THE BREWERY:
FILLING GROWLERS
AND THE LIKE

BEER GEEKS PRIDE THEMSELVES on knowing when to drink a beer. Not the time of day (because the answer is *always*), but the age of a beer. While some beers certainly should be cellared and aged, the vast majority of beers are going to be at their peak of tastiness right when they're released.

For the most part, brewers are the best judges of when a beer should be sent out for purchase. They're intimately familiar with the profile changes a beer undergoes and will release it when it hits its stride. Therefore, procuring beer at the source is an attractive option when the opportunity presents itself.

Breweries with taprooms will occasionally sell bottled and canned versions of their beer, but, in general, Beer Geeks buying beer directly from the source will be doing so with a growler or some kind of similar takeaway container. These containers, which are often glass jugs, let beer drinkers enjoy draft-esque beer in the comfort of their own homes while avoiding outrageous taproom prices and minimizing interaction with the I'm-God's-gift-to-beer-because-I-move-tap-handles-up-and-down bartender.

While Beer Geeks love the growler, they also recognize the shortcomings. Beers are extremely susceptible to oxidation, and when a growler is filled with foaming draft beer, the resulting brew almost certainly has an extra dose of oxygen and reduced carbonation. Additionally, even the geekiest Beer Geek does not clean a growler to the same standards that a brewery does its glassware. This, combined with the somewhat sketchy sanitary conditions of most tap lines, means that the beer is ripe for contamination. Therefore, a Beer Geek will typically drink a growler within a few days of filling it.

Growlers 101

BACK IN THE 1800s, growlers were how home beer drinkers got their beer. The legend goes that the poor-fitting lids often leaked, causing the sloshing beer to make gurgling or "growling" noises during transport, hence the name.

Just a decade ago the only option was the traditional 64-ounce glass jug growler, but entrepreneurs have since created a host of growlers in other shapes and materials, ranging from the awesome-yet-expensive insulated stainless steel Hydroflasks to the hipster-friendly ceramic milk jug. Additionally, smaller 32-ounce growlers have recently burst onto the scene. These "growlettes" (known regionally as *grumblers*, *grenades*, *howlers*, *mini-growlers*, *half-growlers*, *Boston Round*, or *growlitos*) are a popular choice for those lonely Beer Geeks needing only two pints instead of four.

Taproom Limited Releases
SURVIVAL GUIDE

WHILE BREWERY TAPROOMS are usually devoted to growler fills and on-premises pints, occasionally they'll play host to the release of a limited one-off brew. These beers are typically not distributed to stores, bars, or other venues and can be obtained only during these releases. Given the intrinsic small-batch nature and inherent rarity of these beers, they are essentially guaranteed to be delicious and are an obvious draw for any Beer Geek.

However, these events can get a little crazy with Beer Geeks, fanboys/girls, unsuspecting locals, scalpers, and whale traders all vying for the same beer. Additionally, seemingly intelligent breweries continually find new and creative ways to screw up event logistics by underestimating the draw of said beer.

When these releases go well they can be some of the most fun a Beer Geek can have: you get to meet other Beer Geeks and see old friends, all while getting an awesome beer. When they go poorly, though, they can leave a bad taste in your mouth, forever marring the image of a brewery you had revered.

7 TRIED-AND-TRUE TIPS FOR GETTING THE MOST OUT OF A BREWERY RELEASE

1. ALWAYS SHOW UP EARLIER THAN YOU THINK YOU SHOULD. Really. Never underestimate the dedication of your fellow Beer Geeks.

2. FOLLOW THE BREWERY ON SOCIAL MEDIA. Websites, blogs, and feeds are often invaluable sources for any last-minute changes leading up to the event.

3. HAVE CASH ON HAND. Credit card readers can crash, and sometimes cash-only lines will form in order to help avoid impending stampedes.

4. ALWAYS BRING A BOTTLE OR TWO of beer to share while waiting in line, since impromptu bottle shares might sprout up. Be prepared — nobody likes a moocher.

5. HAVE A SMALL TASTING GLASS. Don't get left out of that in-line bottle share.

6. NO CUTSIES — you or your friends. This is always awkward since you'll likely spot old pals while waiting, but nothing ruins a festive mood faster than line cutters.

7. NO MULING. Releases almost always have a per-person limit. Bringing non–Beer Geeks (spouses, relatives, panhandlers, etc.) to boost your allocation is frowned upon. Always think of the guy in line who gets left out because you worked the system.

ONLINE BEER SALES
A LAST RESORT

WHEN A BEER GEEK can't find a beer in her local shops, it's usually because the beer is ultra-rare, is outside of her distribution area, or she lives in a neglected beer locale. While beer trading (more on that later) will solve any of these problems, there is another option for solving the latter two: the online beer shop.

A bevy of websites carry large selections of craft beer. For the most part, these stores have selections similar to that of a decent bottle shop in a major city, but keep in mind that they typically won't have limited releases or ultra-rare beers. Many beer fans get excited when they look at these websites and see that they offer beers from distant breweries like Cigar City. However, further inspection reveals that they only offer their standard six-pack beers, certainly no Hunahpu's or Good Gourd. These sites are looking for high-volume sales, and creating a new webpage for every one-off beer that passes through is way too time-consuming.

Therefore, for Beer Geeks hunting non-rare beers that aren't in their distribution area, the online beer store is a somewhat viable option. The "somewhat" is due to the cost of shipping: Prices vary among websites but are often based on shipping an entire box of beer (usually 12 bottles). Some stores offer "free" shipping when an entire box is ordered, but a quick investigation shows that the transport cost has simply been rolled into the price of the beer, which usually comes out to $3 to $5 a bottle. On the surface, this seems relatively reasonable, until you multiply it by an entire case's worth of bottles.

While high-rolling Beer Geeks might not bat an eye at this expense, most will decide that their local selection of "normal" beers will suffice and reserve their shipping money for trading for whales.

BEER TRADING
THE DARK AND WINDING PATH
TO BANKRUPTCY

IN A BEER GEEK'S RELENTLESS PURSUIT to try every beer produced, it quickly becomes apparent that many beers — even the majority of them — are not available close to home. And like the scent of a condor-egg omelet, such rarity becomes yet another lure.

While the online store is an option for acquiring out-of-market beers, there are simply too many other Beer Geeks gunning for the same beers. And even if a website is able to keep up with demand, that might just mean that the beer is not as good as everyone originally thought. Instead, the bulk of Beer Geeks opt to trade beer with distantly located Beer Geeks. This is typically done through the beer-related websites BeerAdvocate.com and RateBeer.com, both of which have dedicated trading forums.

In general, these forums work on the premise of a prospective trader posting a request that describes a) the beer(s) that they want, and b) the beer(s) they are willing to give up for them. On both websites these forums are called "ISO:FT," an acronym for *In Search Of:For Trade.* When composing the request, the title should be written in this format.

For example, say a Vermont-based Beer Geek is looking to land a Cigar City Hunahpu. Living in Vermont, he should have easy access to Heady Topper, a well-known trade bait. The Beer Geek would begin the trade request with the title:

"ISO: Hunahpu FT: Heady Topper"

Then, in the body of the request, he would list more specific terms, such as:

"8 cans of Heady for one Huna"

Enticing tidbits or alternative trade offers are always welcome ways of fleshing out the offer:

"Just picked up yesterday from the brewery. Super fresh."

"Can also do regular lineup beers from Hill Farmstead."

Anyone interested in the trade then contacts the Beer Geek through the website's private messaging function. Publicly negotiating in the thread is considered poor form (mostly for fear of trade values being publically established; beer traders are very wary of publicizing trade details).

Negotiations can last a few messages or sometimes stretch out for weeks or even months. It is not unusual for the trade to expand to include other beers once a rapport is established. After all, shipping is not cheap (a box shipped domestically starts around $12), and most traders want to make it worth their while.

In addition to the agreed-upon beers, it is customary to throw in a few more bottles as a friendly gesture. These beers are known as "extras" and are an excellent example of what Beer Geekery is all about. The difficulty lies in deciding what *level* of extras to include. Provide too much or too little, and you might end up with an awkward situation where one party feels they didn't send enough. While somewhat clumsy, the fairly typical scenario is to agree to the level of extras in advance. This can be something as simple as, "two to three local beers." It is also perfectly acceptable to agree to omit extras.

Acronym Etiquette

WHILE THERE IS CERTAINLY SPOKEN SLANG in the Beer Geek world, the most prevalent slang is written, largely in acronyms. This is especially true in the online beer community, where acronyms are used extensively. Like in spoken language, this serves to speed up communication and signal a high degree of experience. Acronyms can be tricky, though, and using them incorrectly can result in more damage than good. For guidance, consult the Beer Geek Dictionary (page 188), and always abide by the following five acronym guidelines:

- **KNOW YOUR ACRONYM.** Seems obvious, but referring to Three Floyds as 3F, instead of FFF will earn you an instant noob tattoo.

- **DON'T CREATE ACRONYMS.** You'll only appear to be trying too hard. Acronyms are not coined by anyone; they simply appear out of the Beer Geek ethos.

- **WAIT TO SEE IT AT LEAST TWICE BEFORE USING.** A Beer Geek waits until the necessity of an acronym has been established. Excessive acronyms help no one.

- **NEVER VOCALIZE ACRONYMS,** except in specific instances. Referring to Russian River's Pliny the Younger as "P-T-Y" at the bar should earn you an instant cold shoulder. It is acceptable to vocalize some acronyms (see the Beer Geek Dictionary), but in these cases you must always say the letters (G-A-B-F, not gab-fah).

- **NEVER ASK WHAT AN ACRONYM MEANS.** Except to Google. If you have to ask . . .

Once the terms have been established, both parties then pack up their respective boxes of beer and ship them to each other. The timeframe in which the box will be shipped is generally agreed upon in advance, and a message is sent, along with a tracking number, when it goes out. First-time traders are expected to ship their box first, with the more experienced party following suit once the tracking number has been received. A certain degree of trust is required in shipping a box of rare beer to a relative stranger, and this helps put minds at ease.

DETERMINING TRADE VALUE

To a new trader it may seem daunting to determine what makes a trade offer fair. The best approach is to watch the ISO:FT forum to see what offers are being put up for the beer you're considering. While you probably won't see the actual negotiation, people occasionally post "All set here," or something similar, to let people know when the offer is closed (suggesting that the original offer was not unreasonable). Additionally, lopsided trade offers are usually met with . . . spirited criticism.

When it comes to framing a trade offer there are two schools of thought. Some Beer Geeks opt for the dollar-for-dollar trade, meaning the trade is based on the cost of a beer, not its rarity. This is common for beers that are not super rare but just have a limited distribution area (Heady Topper and Pliny the Elder are good examples). When going the dollar-for-dollar route, it is typical to include "4" in the post to attract likeminded individuals.

> *Dollar-for-dollar traders typically sleep very well at night and have a high opinion of themselves.*

The more common type of trade is based on rarity and known as a "street value" trade. Such trades are more difficult to get a feel for because everyone will have a different opinion of a beer's rarity and value. The best approach in this case is to put your best offer out there and see what kinds of responses come back. The worst that can happen? A torrential onslaught of online shaming for the stupidity of an uneven offer.

The Great Hype Machine

THE TRADE VALUE OF A BEER is based on the amount of hype the beer has received. Therefore, it is always in the trader's interest to make his local, limited-release beers as desirable as possible. When reviewing these beers online, a beer trader will ensure that any flaws are overlooked and strengths magnified. Inquiries as to the availability of the beer are met with claims that it "never even hit the shelves." Especially "industrious" traders working in conjunction will create simulated trade threads to make it appear that these beers have been successfully traded for beers well outside their league, thereby elevating their perceived status. Most in the trading community believe these strategies and techniques were initially perfected in the Chicago beer trading scene (reports of a Chi-town Beer Traders Union have never been verified) and have since been applied elsewhere.

SHIPPING METHODS AND THE LEGALITY OF BEER TRADING

There are a variety of legal concerns involved in the trading of beer. Foremost would seem to be the lack of a state liquor license by either party, which is legally necessary for the transfer of beer. Some argue that since the beer is being traded, not sold, this requirement does not apply, but most would agree that's a stretch at best. Another issue is with each state's alcohol import laws. These laws vary widely, but most don't allow the unlicensed movement of alcohol across state borders without proper tax and duty collection (to determine how serious your state is in this regard, check an online beer store to see if they can ship to your state). In reality, though, the issue that brings beers traders the most anxiety revolves around alcohol shipping methods.

Per the United States Postal Service, it is illegal to use their services to transport alcohol, and, depending on the state, you could be charged with a felony. Basically, no Beer Geek is going to use the USPS to ship a box of beer. The private shipping companies FedEx and UPS are more lax in the sense that it is not necessarily illegal (outside of the import law as mentioned above) to ship alcohol; it's just against their policy. However, according to Beer Geeks who've been unfortunate enough to be caught (leaking boxes are the typical giveaway), the worst-case scenario is that the box will be disposed of and associated account canceled.

To avoid interaction with inquiring clerks, most people create an online account, print out the label at home, and leave the box in the outgoing bin of a drop-off location (such as Kinkos).

If questioned, veteran traders say that sloshing sounds are best explained by saying that you are shipping barbeque marinades (leading FedEx employees across the country to be under the impression that there is a massive movement of marinade aficionados).

The final legal hurdle surrounds the possibility that you are sending alcohol to minors. There is no real way to verify a trading partner's age outside of requiring an adult signature upon delivery, which would surely raise a red flag with the shipping company. Nonetheless, many reason that unless the trading request is for a keg of Keystone or a box of Boone's Farm, a minor already in possession of beer is unlikely to want to trade it for other beer (though weirder things have happened). Either way, providing alcohol to minors is a very serious offense.

With all these legal issues in mind, one might wonder why anyone would ever trade beer. The reality is that hundreds of beer trades go down every day on an easily traceable public forum, leading one to believe that authorities may turn a blind eye to such small-scale infractions. Something like driving 56 in a 55.

TRADER FEEDBACK

Both BeerAdvocate.com and RateBeer.com have forums where you can leave feedback on your experience with a trader. Different forums work slightly differently, but each has a way to track a person's trade history on its profile page, similar to the way eBay does. This provides some guidance when you are choosing potential trading partners.

While trader feedback forums definitely help weed out bad traders, there is always a risk of a trader turning sour and ripping off even the most veteran of traders. One such thing happened on BeerAdvocate.com a few years ago when a well-known, seasoned trader set up a series of concurrent large, high-value trades, received the beer, never shipped on his end, and then disappeared. That is, until a few months later when the beers showed up on eBay. In such cases there isn't really any legal recourse since the whole premise is illegal; it's just an accepted risk.

The **DOS** and **DON'TS** of Beer Trading

DO

DON'T

DO

- **COMMUNICATE** often and promptly.

- **PACK YOUR BOX** excessively well. It should be able to withstand being tossed onto a porch.

- **RESPOND** to each trade offer, be it yes or no.

- **BE HONEST** in the trader feedback forums.

- **USE A RIDICULOUS AMOUNT OF ACRONYMS** and slang in your ISO:FT. It feels too good not to.

- **SET UP** the "extras" expectation in advance.

- **SHIP** quickly.

DON'T

- **CREATE "FEELER" POSTS** with no real intention of trading.

- **BECOME IMPATIENT.** It's okay to wait a couple days for a response (a week is too long, though).

- **BE AFRAID** to say "no thanks" if you get a bad vibe from an offer. Poor grammar and mis-spellings should be judged harshly, as they are an excellent indication of character.

- **TRY TO RIP PEOPLE OFF** with lopsided trades. Beer Geekery is not about trying to get the largest hoard.

- **PROPOSE** auction-type ISO:FTs (i.e., "make me an offer"). It's not about getting the most for the least.

- **THREADJACK.** Specifically, don't try to leach off of someone else's ISO:FT by using their thread to offer the same deal. Set up your own ISO:FT.

- **BACK OUT** once the terms have been agreed upon.

IN-PERSON TRADES AND GROUP TRADES

One way to avoid the legal and shipping hassles of beer trading is to propose an in-person trade. These trades work the same as the shipped-beer trades, as far as posting and negotiating, but the final trade occurs in person (duh). BeerAdvocate.com has a dedicated forum for in-person (IP) trades, while RateBeer.com leaves it up to the poster ("IP Trade" is typically included in the thread title). While in-person trades have their obvious benefits, they're much less popular due to the limited pool of prospective trading partners and the fact that trading partners will typically have access only to beers that you also have access to. However, if you missed out on a local limited release, this is one of the best ways to get a bottle and a good way to meet local Beer Geeks and/or weirdos. In-person trades also work well when vacationing . . . no doubt your spouse will enjoy it.

In addition to beer trading between individuals, there are also "Beer It Forward" trades, in which a group of traders swap beer in a variety of different ways. These trades are set up on the same beer-related websites (BeerAdvocate and RateBeer) as normal ISO:FT trades. A person looking to host the group trade will post a request for participants, along with the general guidelines and trading style.

The various group trading styles are as follows:

- **BIF (BEER IT FORWARD).** The group host sends a box of beer to one of the group members. That member then sends a box of beer to a different group member. This continues until everyone has received a box of beer with the host being the last to receive a box. General box expectations (styles, amounts, etc.) are determined before the BIF begins. In a *shotgun-style* BIF, all box recipients are assigned in advance and sent at the same time.

- **GIF (GROWLER IT FORWARD).** The same as a BIF but with growlers instead of bottles.

- **CIF (CHALICE IT FORWARD).** The same as a BIF but with glassware instead of beer.

- **LIF (LOTTERY IT FORWARD).** This style revolves around a group of traders who send or receive boxes based on the outcome of some sort of event. For example, each member is assigned an NFL team and when their team loses they have to send a box to the victor. Pity the Beer Geek who gets dealt the Jaguars.

- **CHARITY LIF.** Very different from the standard LIF; in the Charity LIF, a box of beer is offered up for lottery by an individual. Many times this is done to raise money for a charity (for example, every $10 donated to St. Judes is an entry to win a box beer). Sometimes Charity LIFs are done without donations, with a generous Beer Geek just looking to make someone's day. This is not exactly a group trade, except in the sense that multiple Beer Geeks are vying to win the box.

THE VALUE OF BEER
LEARNING TO RECOGNIZE (AND DISREGARD) THE $/OZ. AND OTHER METRICS

IT IS AN UNFORTUNATE CIRCUMSTANCE that beer costs money. Because of this, Beer Geeks must always consider a pint's price. This is not to say that Beer Geeks are cheap, actually quite the contrary, but there are (seemingly ever-escalating) limits.

When weighing a beer's price, one must first consider its volume. Ten years ago nearly all beer was served in 16-oz. pints or 12-oz. bottles or cans, but the rise in popularity of the 22-oz. bomber blew the doors off this standard. Bottled and canned beers now regularly come in sizes ranging from the 9-oz. nip to the 375-mL demi bottle, and all the way up to the 32-oz. oil can. And those are just bottles you can get at the store. Once bar owners realized customers would buy beers in sizes other than pints, the onslaught of 10-oz. pours began.

This variance in volume has led to the creation of the **Dollar Per Ounce** metric among Beer Geeks, a relatively straightforward measurement that allows you to easily compare the cost of beers in varying container sizes (similar to the unit pricing you find in the grocery store). Easy enough to crunch while sober, it's perhaps a little tough a few beers in. However, using this metric helps a Beer Geek make sound financial decisions when choosing her beer. For example, let's use it to make a choice among the beers shown on the chart on the facing page.

When you look at this chart, multiple things come to light. For example, if looking for a Flanders red, many will get sticker shock from the Madame Rose, but as you see here it actually comes out to a nearly identical price per ounce when compared to the seemingly more modestly priced Trinity Old Growth. Both of these beers are more than twice the unit price of Rodenbach Grand Cru, a classic Flanders red.

BEER	COST	OUNCES	$/OZ.
Trinity Old Growth	$12	12.7 (375 mL)	$0.94
Goose Island Madame Rose	$25	25.3 (750 mL)	$0.99
Rodenbach Grand Cru	$11	25.3 (750 mL)	$0.43
Cigar City Jai Alai	$10	72 (6-pack)	$0.14
Green Flash IPA	$6	22 (650.6 mL)	$0.27
Orval	$6	11.2 (330 mL)	$0.54
Green Flash Rayon Vert	$3	12 (354.9 mL)	$0.25
Mikkeller 1000 IBU	$13	12.7 (375.6 mL)	$1.02
Cantillon Classic Gueuze	$25	25.3 (750 mL)	$0.99

The chart also shows us that Mikkeller's DIPA, 1000 IBU, is slightly more expensive per ounce than the cult favorite Cantillon Classic Gueuze (if you can find it), which might cause you to scratch your head. And you can see what a bargain six-packs are when comparing Cigar City's beloved Jai Alai IPA to the unit cost of a bomber of Green Flash's IPA. But Green Flash fans fear not, as this measurement also proves that the brewery's homage to Orval, Rayon Vert, is about half the price of the Trappist original.

You don't need a Rainman-esque math mind to come up with these numbers. Instead, simply round the ounces and dollars to the point that they are easily divisible. It just needs to be close enough that you can compare the various options. Suddenly, the seemingly impossible task of picking out a bottle at your local store becomes vastly easier. Sure, that lemur poop–infused AleSmith stout may be getting tons of hype, but $2/oz. is too crazy for most beer shoppers. The key is knowing your $/oz. limits and sticking to them when deciding to splurge on that ultra-rare gem.

Another popular metric is the **Alcohol per Pour**. When faced with a beer menu that has varying pour sizes, it can be tricky to determine exactly how much alcohol you're getting from the different options. While difficult to grasp at first, this measurement cuts out the confusion by figuring how much alcohol is actually in the glass. The formula is as follows:

Alcohol Per Pour = ABV x ounces of pour

Take for example the group of beers on this chart:

BEER	ABV (%)	OZ.	ALCOHOL (OZ.)
Bass Pale Ale	5.0	20	1.0
Sierra Nevada Pale Ale	5.6	16	0.9
Bell's Two Hearted Ale	7.0	16	1.1
Boulevard Wheat	4.4	16	0.7
Dogfish Head 90 Minute	9.0	10	0.9
Boulevard 6th Glass	10.5	12	1.3
Stone Old Guardian	11.0	10	1.1

Initially, many people would think that having two pours of 90 Minute Double IPA would make you more tipsy than two English pints of Bass, but as shown above, they'd be wrong (though not by much). You can also see that a pint of Bell's Two Hearted IPA, with its sneakily high ABV, actually packs the same punch per pour as Stone's bruising Old Guardian barleywine.

At first glance, this measurement appears to be about the quickest way to get drunk, a sort of lush statistician's tool, but really it should be used to make educated session-drinking decisions. While some may always go for the highest alcohol/pour option, others will instead choose the opposite because they are looking to enjoy more than one beer without being overwhelmed by the effect of the alcohol.

Now, those looking to get the most "bang" for their buck will want to compare the Alcohol Per Pour outcome with the cost of the pour. The result is the **SUGS** (Sauced-Up Geek Statistic) rating:

SUGS = cost ÷ alcohol per pour

Using the same beer list as the previous chart, but this time including prices, the following chart gives the SUGS ratings:

BEER	COST($)	ALCOHOL (OZ.)	SUGS
Bass Pale Ale	$4	1.0	4.0
Sierra Nevada Pale Ale	$3	0.9	3.3
Bell's Two Hearted Ale	$5	1.1	4.6
Boulevard Wheat	$5	0.7	7.1
Dogfish Head 90 minute	$8	0.9	8.9
Boulevard 6th Glass	$6	1.3	4.6
Stone Old Guardian	$6	1.1	5.5

The lower the SUGS, the cheaper it is to get a buzz. I'll have a Sierra Nevada Pale, please.

You might imagine that these calculations would require a normal Beer Geek to carry a calculator into the bar or bottle shop. However, Beer Geeks do no such thing. Rather, they develop a sort of sixth sense for these metrics, subconsciously doing the calculations in their heads. This gives them one more tool in their bag full of tricks, enabling them to pick out the gems from overpriced beer menus.

BREWERANIA
COASTERS, SIGNS, AND OTHER JUNK

THE RECLUSE BEER GEEK is nearly a nonentity. A huge part of living the beery life is sharing experiences with like-minded individuals. So, after an especially rare beer or exceptional brewery visit, it's natural to want to document the occasion with some sort of keepsake, like a trophy to prove the pinnacle achieved in your beer education:

Just a few years back you might have collected empty bottles or coasters to remember the event, but in today's digital world the experience is usually documented by uploading photos to Facebook or "checking in" a beer on the mobile app *UnTappd*.

There remains a sect of Beer Geekery that continues to collect mementos and display them like animal heads in a safari trophy room.

Members of this group are often unmarried and have a penchant for movie-poster home décor. These Beer Geeks can be identified by their bookshelves of empty bottles, vintage beer trays, and tin brewery signs. Inevitably, large collections of bottle caps and corks can be found squirreled away in closets in preparation for a grandiose project involving epoxy and some sort of home bar that does not yet exist but which is guaranteed to be "epic."

There is an element of Brewerania required of all Beer Geeks, however, and that is brewery apparel. At any beer-centric social function, it is expected that Beer Geeks will adorn themselves in either a hat or shirt that displays how seriously they take beer. While it may look like bragging to the outside observer, the clothing's function is actually two-fold:

1. to act as a conversational icebreaker, and

2. to be a signal flare of sorts, helping real Beer Geeks, mixed in a sea of the uninitiated, home in on one another.

BEER GEEK
ESSENTIALS

THOUGH EXCESS PARAPHERNALIA is seen as gauche, the essentials (select beers, glassware, and works of literature) are, well, essential. A true Beer Geek always has the following necessities on hand.

REQUISITE GLASSWARE

As previously discussed, while Glass Snobs put their efforts into always matching a beer to its brewery's glassware, Beer Geeks instead spend their time and money on actual beer. Even so, at least four of each of these classics should be represented in your home:

 **TULIP.** The standard glass. Its lipped, concave shape strikes the perfect balance between aroma-heightening and drinkability.

 **WEISS GLASS.** This tall, sexy style maximizes head retention and aesthetics and facilitates high-volume swilling. Used for sessionable or warm-weather beers.

 **SHAKER (PINT) GLASS.** Used for rinse water during beer tastings or when drinking BMC (or similar) beers, where minimal taste experience is preferred.

 SNIFTER. Used for high-ABV sipping beers, like vintage barleywines and Belgian quads, where the aroma is just as important as the taste.

ESSENTIAL CELLAR STOCK

Any self-respecting Beer Geek recognizes that certain beers benefit from a stint in the cellar. Aging beer at one's home signals your level of knowledge and commitment to fermented malt beverages. A standard cellar will include:

- ◊ **AMERICAN BARLEYWINE.** Too hoppy to be worth aging for a long period of time, but six months to two years will mellow the booziness while still maintaining a lupulin bouquet. The classic choice is Sierra Nevada Bigfoot.

- ◊ **ENGLISH BARLEYWINE.** With deep sherry notes, a cornucopia of dried fruit, and hints of Churchill's armchair, there is not a more cellar-worthy beer. Vintage bottles of Thomas Hardy's Ale are required, along with J. W. Lees.

- ◊ **IMPERIAL STOUT.** As with American barleywines, aging potential is limited, but a year or two mellows the astringent roasted notes into black chocolate deliciousness. Barrel-aged versions are preferred for their greater complexity.

- ◊ **BELGIAN QUAD.** The barleywine of Brussels. Over time, the hot, spicy yeast notes melt into vanilla, caramel, and raisins. Like English barleywines, the authentically sourced versions (Rochefort, Achel, De Struise) are favorites. At least one bottle of the rare Westvleteren 12 should be kept on hand and, if requested, happily opened as though it's an everyday brew.

- ◊ **FLANDERS RED.** Almost always pasteurized prior to bottling, this sour beer takes on rich oxidative (caramel, fig, sherry) notes over time. Vintage bottles are the go-to option for visiting wine snobs who insist they're "just not into beer."

- ◊ **GUEUZE.** No beer cellar is complete without a strong presence of Beer Geek champagne (a case of 750-mL bottles minimum). Ages gracefully and delicately for decades.

- ◊ **BORDEAUX,** or similar tannic-rich wine; one or two bottles. This conveys that you understand and appreciate that wine is age-worthy but that you consider beer the superior cellar stock. *"Oh sure, I age wine too, but beer is just so much more complex."*

MANDATORY LIBRARY

The hallmark of a Beer Geek is a deep understanding of the crafting and makeup of all things beer. A library of beer literature is required for referencing and as a display of your dedication:

- *The Complete Joy of Homebrewing.* Homebrewer or not, you'll find this classic guide by Charlie Papazian delivers brewing know-how in an easy-to-understand format.

- *The Oxford Companion to Beer.* The ultimate beer book. Essential info on everything beer-related, written by the experts. Its hefty price tag tells everyone you're a connoisseur.

- *Tasting Beer.* Randy Mosher's classic guide to drinking beer. A Beer Geek's life truly begins only after reading this book.

- *Vintage Beer.* Everything you need to know about stocking and enjoying your cellar. Written by the world's most fascinating, and most humble, beer writer.

- *Wild Brews.* Provides a technical understanding of lambic beers and beyond. By Jeff Sparrow.

- *Radical Brewing.* Despite a disturbing amount of vintage-beer-coaster porn, this quintessential book on brewing techniques, also by Randy Mosher, covers nearly every beer style.

- *Yeast.* Chris White's (of White Labs fame) masterwork on the microbiological workhorse responsible for beer.

- *LambicLand.* The ultimate guide — including production, tasting, and visiting notes — to the Beer Geek's most sought-after beer style.

- *Good Beer Guide Belgium.* The only guidebook needed during the ultimate beercation.

FRIDGE FODDER

A Beer Geek's refrigerator has beer at the ready for any situation that may arise. A typical inventory:

- Six-pack or bomber of an IPA less than one month old

- Five-pack of BMC left by non–Beer Geek friends from your last party (offered only to stubborn BMC devotees and always as a last option)

- 750-mL bottle of vintage gueuze on deck for impromptu celebration

- Bomber of barrel-aged strong beer (barleywine, imperial stout, etc.)

- Six-pack of local, sessionable, craft ale

- Aecht Schlenkerla Rauchbier (or similar smoked beer) for a beery marinade

- Cheese pairings: a vintage cheddar, a funky blue, and a soft, mild goat cheese

CHAPTER 5
DRINKING

To put it mildly, Beer Geeks are particular about the beer they drink. They don't waste time, money, and liver capacity on bad beer, and they put a formidable amount of thought into the beer they consume. But consume they do, and impressively well.

LUCKILY, THE ERA OF HAVING TO HUNT far and wide for a bar or restaurant with a decent beer list is becoming a thing of the past. Sometimes you can even find good beer at places that used to be beery wastelands, like airports, concert venues, and sporting events. And let's not forget the magic of the beer festival, where everyday beer drinkers get caught up in the wave of beery amazingness and start down the path to becoming full-fledged Beer Geeks.

Nevertheless, the at-home beer-drinking scene with its bottle shares and blind tastings will always be the domain of hardcore Beer Geeks. Only here can geeks truly geek out — and, say, split a bottle 15 ways before engaging in an adjective-fueled pissing match. *Mmm, Hungarian late-harvest currants . . .*

Let the following chapter be your guide to drinking like a Beer Geek, wherever you happen to be.

BARS
TYPES AND STRENGTHS

BEER GEEKS ARE FOREVER SEEKING craft beer in bars across America. And as craft beers, with their superior flavor (and higher price), slowly become accepted by the masses, the choices are constantly improving.

In most major cities it is no longer unusual to find bars devoted solely to craft beer with nary a BMC on tap,

and Beer Geeks will always search out these establishments.

However, it remains an unfortunate truth that the vast majority of bars still treat craft beer as a hoity-toity afterthought, if they consider it at all. So, when you find yourself faced with the following bar types, use this handy guide to navigate your way through.

BEER BAR. Wonderful establishments built by and for Beer Geeks. This is where Beer Geeks can ask annoying questions about a beer's production size, ingredients, or serving temperature — and get enthusiastic responses rather than confounded, annoyed dismissals. Beers are kept at the proper temperature, tap lines are immaculately clean, the draft list is ever-rotating, and the bottle list includes vintages. If any of these things are not true, it is not a *beer bar*, and an alternate drinking destination should be considered.

The Bottle Shop Bar

THE BOTTLE SHOP BAR is a subset of the beer bar. Certain states that have wonderful liquor laws allow liquor store customers to drink their purchases in-store. While this may conjure up images of bums chugging forties in the strip mall liquor store, what it usually looks like is a high-end bottle shop with a "half" bar. This is a fantastic thing for a Beer Geek because the options are probably light-years better than at your average bar, plus you can visually peruse your choices. On top of that, prices are going to be that of a liquor store (some charge a small corkage fee), enabling one to sample on the cheap. If we could all be so lucky . . .

HIPSTER BAR. Typically disguised as a dive bar but easily identified by the presence of vegan baked goods, fixed-gear bicycles, and the wearing of knit hats in the summer. Lovers of everything craft and homegrown, these bars are far from the worst choice and usually have a handful of local options. But don't expect great things, as the average patron is not looking for much depth in his suds.

COLLEGE BAR. College bars vary greatly depending on locale. Certainly your average college bar in Fort Collins, Colorado, is going to have a superior selection to one in Gainesville, Florida. That said, even in the best of college bars, the taps are going to be limited to the local session offerings (Fat Tire in Fort Collins, for example). Beer Geeks won't typically frequent such venues, but the saving grace of the college bar is its seeming disregard for the craft beer pricing premium. It is only at these establishments that blanket specials like $2 beers or 2-for-1 pints are offered regardless of the chosen beer. A Beer Geek never turns down a $5 pitcher of Odell's IPA.

....

SPORTS BAR. A large category ranging from the cleavage chains to the ubiquitous strip mall locale. Many Beer Geeks have a shared love of sporting events and beer and will therefore find themselves at such establishments frequently. While no limited release or specialty tap beers will be available, most places have a decent craft selection. However, be wary that glass sizes usually come in either the ridiculous "large" (25+ oz.) or the more appropriate "small" (12 to 16 oz.) sizes. Beer Geeks, with their understanding of how beer flavors change as a beer warms, always order the appropriate size.

*Also, beware that this is the favorite hiding spot
of the dreaded frosted mug.*

....

BREWPUB. A very large contingent but also a slowly shrinking one. In the '90s, when people were still unwilling to spend a large premium on well-crafted beers, new brewers felt compelled to offer full food service to help pay the bills. But in today's brave new beer world, the sky is seemingly the limit as to what the public is willing to pay for a pint, and brewers now easily cover the mortgage on beer alone. Most brewpubs still around are holdovers from the old era and typically known as restaurants rather than breweries. Beers are usually limited to the omnipresent WASP selection (Wheat, Amber, Stout, Pale) and are all too forgettable.

....

FAUX IRISH/BRITISH PUB. Decades ago, these cookie-cutter pubs were the only salvation of pioneering Beer Geeks. This was back when the tiny bit of flavor found in the three or four factory-brewed UK/Irish options were a welcome alternative to, well, the complete lack of flavor found in American factory-brewed beer.

Nowadays, having Guinness on tap impresses nobody, and only a fraction of these bars have embraced craft beer. In general, the majority should be avoided, or at least not sought out for any kind of real beer selection. If you find yourself in such an establishment, inquire if they have any Chimay Red, which for some odd reason always seems to have squirreled its way into these places.

AIRPORT BAR. Typically the domain of sugary sweet, terrifyingly neon cocktails; beer options are often very limited. There is BMC of course, and the ubiquitous Samuel Adams Boston Lager (it's apparently an FAA violation to operate an airport bar without it). You may even be lucky enough to find the blandest offering from the largest local craft brewery, but that's about all a Beer Geek can hope for. In other words, grim stuff. There are a few exceptions, though, and the best approach to locating these establishments is to search the BeerAdvocate.com forums, as the question has been answered by the locals for just about every major US airport. Look for brewery tap houses, especially in beer-loving regions (Rocky Mountains, Pacific Northwest), but don't get too excited, as most only offer their flagship lineup (I'm looking at you, New Belgium Hub). If all else fails, you can sometimes find decent options at higher-end food establishments.

Notable Airport Brewery Taprooms

- *San Diego:* Stone Brewing Co.
- *Portland:* Rogue Ales Public House
- *Tampa:* Cigar City Brewing
- *Denver:* New Belgium Hub
- *Cleveland:* Great Lakes Brewing Company
- *Atlanta:* Sweetwater Draft House and Grill
- *Chicago (O'Hare):* Goose Island Beer Company

HOTEL BAR. A similar situation to the airport bar, as far as selection goes. In reality, though, most Beer Geeks rarely experience the hotel bar, since they are presumably traveling to a city with a different regional distribution than their home area. This means they will instead be at a local beer bar trying out new beers, or in their hotel room, drinking beer that they scored at the local bottle shop (and couldn't fit in their luggage).

....

REDNECK BAR. Drink bourbon.

DIVE BAR. When considering dive bars (real dive bars, not the hip imitations), choices are about as slim as it gets. Craft options are nonexistent and inquiring after them will usually only earn you an icy stare.

A Beer Geek finding himself at a dive bar uses it as a good excuse to become reacquainted with BMC, if only to remind himself why he might spend $20 on a bottle of good beer.

....

NIGHTCLUB. Leave. If bound and chained, drink scotch.

Tap Takeovers: Christmas on a Tuesday

IN A FULL-COURT-PRESS PROMOTIONAL EFFORT (and to reward loyal bar owners), breweries sometimes have a "tap takeover" at a beer bar, putting five or so kegs of their own beer on tap at the same time in an attempt to lure local Beer Geeks. The taps usually include two or three ultra-rare small kegs in addition to one or two run-of-the-mill offerings, and they are frequently available as a flight (a small pour of each beer).

The rare offerings are often very rare, so these takeovers offer a great opportunity to try a handful of specialty beers for a relative bargain. Brewery reps are usually on hand at these events, and schwag flows freely. To take full advantage of the draw, bar owners usually host a takeover on a weekday when they wouldn't otherwise have a large crowd.

BREWERY TAPROOMS
AND TOURS
YET ANOTHER MASH TUN

BEER GEEKS NATURALLY GRAVITATE toward breweries. A powerful siren call draws them in with the promise of beer fresh from the source and the possibility of taproom-exclusive brews. However, there aren't a lot of other reasons for a Beer Geek to visit a brewery. In almost all circumstances, engaging in brewery tours or drinking beers from their normal lineup are activities considered the domain of tourists and noobs.

Standard beers that are normally distributed should be avoided at all costs, as drinking these would defeat the purpose of visiting the brewery. When choosing a beer at a brewery taproom it is imperative that a Beer Geek identify and order the rarest offering available. Well-respected breweries recognize this and have a variety of taproom exclusives on hand at all times. The notable exceptions to this rarity rule are hoppy beers. Given the fleeting nature of hops, incredibly fresh (days-old) versions of IPAs are unique to the same (but less fresh) IPAs bought in a liquor store, making them taproom exclusives in essence, even if their less-fresh versions are not particularly rare.

Breweries Known for Taproom-Only Beers

- **The Bruery** (Placentia, CA)
- **Odell Brewing Co.** (Fort Collins, CO)
- **Kuhnhenn Brewing Co.** (Warren, MI)
- **Jackie O's** (Athens, OH)
- **Cigar City Brewing** (Tampa, FL)

As for brewery tours, though they may seem appealing in theory, you will quickly discover that almost all of them consist of 20 to 30 minutes of viewing large conical metal structures. As a rule, tours are led by the employee with the least amount of knowledge of the brewery's beer and brewing practices. Participants often see the tour as the perfect opportunity to regale tour mates of the tales of the time they "got so drunk off [*insert brewery's flagship beer*] . . ." and did something really dumb. The token homebrewer is a familiar fixture on such tours and, in an effort to ensure the entire group grasps the depth of his brewing knowledge, constantly badgers the unaware tour guide over the technical details of the various conical metal structures.

The Beer Geek knows the best use of the brewery tour is solely to remove the riffraff from the taproom, if only for a short while.

NON-DISTRIBUTING NEIGHBORHOOD BREWERIES

The last couple of years have seen the emergence of a new breed of brewery that relies solely on on-premises sales. These breweries are often homebrewers-turned-pro enterprises that specialize in everyday drinkable offerings very similar to what was seen in the '90s brewpubs: amber, wheat, pale, stout. They typically have no plans to grow much beyond being a neighborhood pub and are content with these run-of-the-mill selections. Beer Geeks appreciate and sometimes frequent these establishments but spend little time thinking about or promoting such ventures. There certainly are some notable exceptions, such as Peg's Cantina in Gulfport, Florida, known for creating world-class barrel-aged stouts.

Acceptable Brewery Tours

....

WHILE BEER GEEKS AVOID most tours, there are some exceptions.

1. BREWERIES THAT UTILIZE KOELSCHIPS. These large, shallow open vessels are used for spontaneous fermentation (inoculating lambics, for example). There is nothing more seductive to Beer Geeks than this process, and viewing the large rectangular metal structure fills an otherwise empty void in their beery lives.

2. TOURS THAT INCLUDE A TRIP TO A BARREL-AGING ROOM. The fact that the brewery even has this room immediately indicates that it is well respected by Beer Geeks (barrels in the corner of the brew house don't count). A Beer Geek's attraction to the barrel room is not tied so much to viewing the wooden vessels but rather to the possibility that the tour guide might decide to pull a small sample directly from a barrel for the group to taste. The allure of getting to say, "Yeah, it's good, but you should try it straight from the barrel" is strong enough to make even the most jaded Beer Geek tolerate a tour or two at the right brewery.

RESTAURANTS
DRINKING BEER WITH THE KIDDOS

BEER GEEKS REQUIRE BEER. And they're human, so they require food too. Therefore, it's inevitable that the two needs will cross paths and some beer drinking will occur at restaurants. And for Beer Geeks who have begun raising a brood of future Beer Geeks, finding a family restaurant that serves good beer may be their only chance to get out into the world of draft beer and taste the latest and greatest trends.

While a tiny handful of restaurants have long given beer its due, it's only more recently that restaurants countrywide have begun to see the light. For older restaurants, the timeworn standard of five rather sorry options (three of which are BMC) is slowly falling to the wayside, and many now have the same number of beer options as wine. Quite a few newer restaurants are wisely putting considerable effort into catering to the ever-growing (and demanding) Beer Geek Nation.

This change comes out of a hard-fought and long-waged battle on the part of elder Beer Geeks who refused to be limited to enjoying quality craft beer only at a bar. Because they incessantly inquired after decent beer choices and refused to settle for factory-made lagers, we are now able to partake of craft beer while enjoying a good meal at a restaurant. That said, there is still some distance to go, and even more so when it comes to the knowledge of the waitstaff.

An incredible tap list is useless if consumers can't find anyone to inform them about it.

In this awkward teenage love affair between restaurant owners and craft beer, navigating the restaurant beer list brings up a whole new host of issues . . .

THE SERVER

While a bartender typically takes a standoffish approach to your beer selection, servers are often much more proactive. They see this as their opportunity to blow your assumedly feeble mind with their imposing beer knowledge. While this is not such a bad thing if you have an informed server, informed servers are unfortunately very few and far between. (Note: A Beer Geek always thanks and tips these rare servers handsomely.)

Instead, inquiring patrons are often offered such gems as:
  It's brewed with Cascade hops to give it a bourbon-like flavor.
Or, when asked about the style of a beer,
  It's an ale, so it's between a craft beer and a lager.
Or the ever-enlightening,
  It's a microbrew, so it's kind of like an IPA.

While dealing with this kind of server can sometimes be taxing, the apathetic alternative is much worse. Annoyed by your audacity in wanting to know what beers are available, these servers will often only mention the few BMC options they've heard of. When asked about the other taps/bottles (in plain view at the bar), their bewildered reply is:
  Oh, those are microbrews. I'd have to try and find a bartender to see what they are.

Which is then followed by an awkward pause as they silently dare you to ask them to do just that.

THE MENU

Since most restaurants are not in the habit of changing their menu daily or weekly, they have a difficult time conveying the beer selection to the consumer. Ideally they would have a regularly updated separate menu, but many places take one of the following approaches instead:

◊ *A chalkboard above the bar* listing all available options, requiring you to get up and awkwardly peer over a bar occupant's shoulders. Given the impeccable artistry put into the chalking, the board is frequently out of date. No good.

◊ *Usage of vague menu placeholders* like "Seasonal Tap" or "Rotating Selection." This approach has led many non–Beer Geeks across the country to think that Seasonal or Rotating is actually a beer style. ("Have you had that Sweetwater Seasonal? It's amazing.") It is a clear indicator that the establishment does not give much consideration to beer and is a disservice to breweries and craft-beer drinkers alike.

◊ *No menu at all,* instead relying on the server to memorize the options. Tap list inquiries are usually met with the ever-infuriating, "What kinds of beer do you like?" (Imagine having to ask what is on the "food menu" and being asked the same thing.) The next step is for the server to rattle off a long, rhythmic chant of all the beer selections (a miserable experience for patrons and servers alike). If the chant starts with them looking at the ceiling and uttering the words "Bud, Bud Light, Coors, Coors Light . . . ," it's a Beer Geek's cue to order water or bourbon.

If you run into a less-than-ideal server, improve your chances of landing a decent beer by visiting the bar itself, inquiring with the bartender, and peeking at any glass-fronted fridges. When you run into a great server, queries about "off-the-menu" or "just tapped" beers can often result in some pleasant surprises.

The "Seasonal" Red Flag

THE WORD *seasonal* is an establishment's way of saying, "Whatever random keg our beer distributor pawns off on us." Since the restaurant does not take beer seriously, the servers rarely do either, often resulting in much questioning as to what exactly the seasonal is. The conversation might go as follows.

> *Beer Geek:* "What is your seasonal?"
> *Server:* "It's a Belgian beer."
> *Beer Geek:* "Okay . . . which beer from Belgium?"
> *Server (confusedly, after a long visit to the bar):* "It's called Bike Tire, it's like an ale. Kind of like a microbrew."
> *Beer Geek:* "You mean Fat Tire?"
> *Server:* "Uh, yeah, that's it. One of those?"

THE PAIRING

Simply put, a great beer restaurant has a great beer list. But only those in the highest echelon of Beer Geek restaurants go the extra step and thoughtfully pair beers with food dishes. These prized locales often suggest beers with each dish (many have beer sommeliers to guide diners in their pairings), and it is quite normal for beer to be used in the cooking process.

However, these restaurants are extremely rare (mmmm, rare), and Beer Geeks must always beware those that blindly offer pairing suggestions with seeming randomness (e.g., Shock Top Honeycrisp Apple Wheat with the baked mac 'n' cheese). Likewise, some restaurants will use beer in the cooking of a dish just for the sake of mentioning it on the menu — a dangerous practice, as hop bitterness presents culinary challenges to the uninitiated.

A Beer Geek knows the general ins and outs of food and beer pairings and can easily spot such ruses (which most commonly occur at '90s-era brewpubs).

THE BASICS OF
BEER AND FOOD PAIRING

WHILE THE REST OF THE WORLD assumes that a meal is always paired with wine, Beer Geeks understand that beer — with its vast range of flavors and aromas, as well as the palate-cleansing advantages of carbonation — is actually the ultimate pairing beverage. Entire books have been written on the subject of pairing food with beer. While it may initially seem a daunting subject to learn, a bit of inspection reveals that there are really just a few general rules that guide most pairing decisions.

It is vital for Beer Geeks to know these rules, as they must be able to apply them not only for their own benefit but, more importantly, to help turn the uninitiated on to good beer. For many a non–beer drinker the idea of beer is still the BMC they shotgunned in college, but a well-paired beer with a meal can often provide the light-bulb moment that leads to becoming a Beer Geek.

Even a Beer Geek's beer-drinking friends will lean on them for suggestions when presented with an overwhelming list of choices at a beer-centric restaurant. This is an important task that requires preparation.

FOOD AND BEER PAIRING GUIDELINES TO WIN FRIENDS AND INFLUENCE PEOPLE

1. **Go the harmonizing route:** Pair a beer's dominant flavors with those of the food. Pair a dark-roasted stout with dark Belgian chocolate, or use the saaz hop–induced spiciness of a Czech pilsner to bring out the heat of a Thai noodle bowl.

2. **Or go the contrast route:** An equally accepted method that instead uses the central characteristic of a beer to contrast with the food. For example, use the acidity of a gueuze to cut through the rich creaminess of a soft sheep's milk cheese, or tame the umami richness of bacon with the roasted bitterness of a coffee stout.

3. **Always match strength with strength:** Be it hop bitterness, alcohol strength, or acidity, it is important to match that characteristic with the dominant aspect of a meal. The subtleties of a kolsch are best paired with a light vinaigrette salad, while the intense hop bitterness of a DIPA can go toe to toe with the strong tanginess of an aged blue cheese.

4. **Confidence is key:** In the end, astute Beer Geeks are well aware that these first three guidelines cover all manner of sins, making it possible to have a basis to pair almost any beer with any food. It's all about picking a guideline and sticking to your choice with confidence. Luckily, beer and food pair so well together it's hard to go wrong.

BEER FESTIVALS
GEEKING AMIDST THE DEBAUCHERY

BEER FESTIVALS, when done right, are the ultimate experience for Beer Geeks. They offer the opportunity to try new beers, connect with fellow Beer Geeks, and network with brewers and brewery reps. And the ability to try a massive number of beers while still maintaining one's geekiness is an art that must be mastered by every Beer Geek.

There are a lot of great festivals out there, but more recently a lot of not-so-great festivals have appeared on the scene too. What used to be mostly the domain of Beer Geeks has since become one of the most popular kinds of events in the United States. While this is great for helping to spread the beer gospel, it has also led to an overall decline in the quality of beers that breweries bring to festivals, since brewers have had to become much choosier about where they send their exciting limited-release beers. Look to these festival types for a good chance of Beer Geek success:

◊ BREWERY FESTIVALS *Highly Regarded by Beer Geeks*

Larger breweries often have festivals on their grounds once a year, or to celebrate an anniversary. Beer selections are bountiful and include vintage offerings, barrel-aged variations, and one-off specialties. These events offer great opportunities to meet brewers and brewery reps, and they're usually very reasonably priced.

◊ BAR FESTIVALS *Top Tier*

It's rather uncommon given the logistical challenges, but beercentric bars will sometimes have festivals on-location. These festivals are usually exceptional, since the organizing bars do the beer purchasing and therefore choose only the best (plus, they are organized by industry Beer Geeks). Notable examples are the Delilah's Vintage Strong Beer Fest in Chicago, Ebenezer's Belgian Beer Festival in Maine, and the Toronado Barleywine Festival in San Francisco.

◦ INVITATIONAL FESTIVALS *Beer Geek Heaven*

Invitationals tend to be collaborative efforts between various brewers looking to showcase their talents. The fact that it gives them a tax-deductible excuse to fraternize is mere coincidence. Contrary to most fests, the actual brewers are usually pouring the beer, and offerings are typically excellent. Notable examples are What the Funk in Denver, Culmination in Anchorage, Extreme Beer Fest in Boston, and the Firestone Walker Invitational in Paso Robles.

◦ THE GREAT AMERICAN BEER FESTIVAL (GABF)
In a Category by Itself

Held every year in Denver in a space that could fit multiple Costcos, this festival boasts brewery numbers hovering around a mindboggling 700. Beer Snobs consider it overdone and lament about how it was *in their day*, but Beer Geeks know better. This is a highly advanced festival that requires careful preparation, strategizing, and training. A mandatory check box on a Beer Geek's bucket list.

STEPS FOR OPTIMIZING THE FESTIVAL EXPERIENCE

1. When considering attending a festival, Beer Geeks begin by researching the festival's list of participating breweries (serious festivals also include a list of beers to be poured). They will then assemble a list of beers of interest and make a quick mental calculation to determine the value of each beer (based on what it would cost to purchase or trade for them). If the value of the beer exceeds that of the ticket price, a Beer Geek will attend. If there are out-of-distribution DONGs on the list, festival attendance is a no-brainer.

2. Once it's been decided that the festival is worth attending, a Beer Geek will assemble a group of fellow Beer Geeks, numbering no greater than eight, to go together. Any larger and the group is too cumbersome to accommodate serious tasting.

3. For large festivals, a strategizing session is held among the fellowship of Beer Geeks to create a prioritized list of breweries to hit once inside. Popular breweries will be hit hard at the onset, since it is not unusual for rare selections to run out in even the first hour. Breweries such as these make up the priority list.

4. Beer Geeks always arrive at the festival with a full stomach, preferably of cheese or other fatty foods, slowing alcohol absorption to maximize allowable intake.

5. Once inside, the priority list is executed. The tasting format is often limited to 1- or 2-oz. samples. When sampling breweries have a line, a Beer Geek never camps out at the front in an attempt to sample multiple beers. This is a classic noob move and goes against all Beer Geek etiquette. Once you get your sample, head immediately to the end of the line to get another sample. Time is of the essence.

6. Fraternizing can fully commence once the priority list has been addressed. At this point, the tasting should move to "free-form format" based upon suggestions from fellow Beer Geeks. It is now okay to talk with brewers and brewery reps, since by this point all festival attendees have had ample opportunity to sample their top beers.

7. As the festival winds down, the Beer Geeks quickly become distinguishable from the posers. While Beer Geeks might certainly get drunk at a festival (there can be a lot of beers to sample, after all), they don't go there with the primary intention of getting drunk. At this stage, non–Beer Geeks begin flinging coasters, knocking their buddy's glass out of his hand, and stealing every bit of brewery schwag not nailed down. Beer Geeks, having properly trained for the event, maintain (some) composure.

8. Once last call goes out, a Beer Geek, knowing full well that the remaining samples being poured aren't any Gold Medal winners, heads out to grab a cab or a bite, leaving the frat pack to do shots of every beer left standing.

Recognize Volunteers vs. Brewery Employees

DEPENDING ON THE FESTIVAL, beers may be poured by brewers and brewery reps or by festival volunteers, or sometimes even a combination of the two. Learning to identify a volunteer (look for clues like a volunteer nametag or shirt) will help you avoid the mistake of asking brewery-specific questions to random strangers who are almost never able to answer them anyway. Seemingly simple, but frequently flubbed.

The Great American Beer Festival
SURVIVAL GUIDE

THE GREAT AMERICAN BEER FESTIVAL is the granddaddy of all the beer festivals and occurs every year in Denver. While not an intimate affair by any means, it affords the Beer Geek the opportunity to taste beer from more than 700 breweries and must be attended at least once in a Beer Geek's lifetime. Pulling off a successful festival experience takes special advance planning. Use the following tips to help maximize your trip to the world's greatest beer spectacle.

PREPARATION

Preparation starts in July when the tickets go on sale. Tickets are sold over two days, the first being limited to an American Homebrewers Association (AHA) member presale. The presale is essential because the sale to the general public sells out almost immediately, allowing only the fastest CAPTCHA code typers through. Membership with the AHA runs around $40 but comes with all sorts of other advantages, from discounts at almost every US brewery to a subscription to *Zymurgy* to reduced GABF ticket prices. Be sure to sign up for your AHA membership at least a week prior to the presale date to ensure processing time. Once you have your tickets, you can start planning in earnest:

1. Decide which session(s) you are attending:

- *Thursday evening:* Many Beer Geeks' favorite. The crowd is limited to those serious enough to take Friday off from work. Additionally, as the first session, all beers are guaranteed to be available.

- *Friday evening:* A respectable session, especially for those who can't weasel the day off from work. Has the benefit of allowing better strategizing, since the pour lists at most breweries are posted by then on the GABF website. Most beer still available.

- *Saturday afternoon:* Also known as the Member's Session as it is limited to only AHA members. Attendance is capped at a lower number, and the brewer or brewery rep is pouring the beer at most booths. This session has a decidedly more sophisticated air. The tasting glasses are made from actual glass rather than plastic, and many breweries reserve special beer selections just for this occasion. The most popular choice of Beer Geeks.

- *Saturday evening:* A drunken shitshow. The domain of roving packs of bros and convicts. Notorious for not having any of the decent beer left. Most brewers and brewery reps have left the building by this session. Avoided by Beer Geeks.

2. Determine your length of stay. The entire week prior to the festival plays host to a ridiculous number of beer events throughout town. It's a Beer Geek fantasy land. Plan to stay for as much of it as you can afford.

3. If traveling from out of town, begin booking flights and hotel rooms as early as possible. Downtown lodging is expensive and goes very quickly; however, the saving grace is Denver's clunky light rail system with its stop right at the Convention Center. This allows attendees to look for non-downtown hotels with easy access to this transportation system to save a bit of money.

4. During the months leading up to the event keep your eyes peeled to the interwebs for brewery lists, pour lists, and the floor plan. Develop a priority list and map. Commit it to memory and have your significant other regularly quiz you. Warily utilize the Brewer's Association GABF app, which has had a shaky-at-best (both signal and operation) performance in the past.

THE DAY ARRIVES

On the day of the festival, you have two choices. The first is to arrive two hours early to get in the front of the line. Experience has shown, however, that this will gain you only about 20 extra minutes inside. The other option is to show up around ten minutes prior, and while the length of the line (which wraps around a city block) is a terrifying sight, it moves unexpectedly fast. Whichever you choose, while waiting eat approximately a pound of cheese to slow alcohol absorption. Then you'll be ready:

1. Once inside, take just a moment to absorb the insane size of the festival.

2. Stick to that priority list, and maintain the willpower to not be led astray.

3. Once the list is achieved, get a bite to eat at one of the various food outlets. Then use the rest of the time to visit random breweries, meet fellow Beer Geeks, and generally be happily reminded of why you became a geek in the first place.

4. The bathroom line is startlingly long but moves quickly. Get a barley-wine to sip on, and have patience.

5. Once last call is made, beeline it out of the festival to beat the masses to wherever it is you're going (taxi stand, light rail, Falling Rock barstool, etc.).

HOSTING A
BEER TASTING ...
WITH STYLE AND GRACE

A CRITICAL SKILL FOR A BEER GEEK to learn is how to flawlessly pull off a beer tasting. For a tasting to be successful, it must be presented as a low-key affair (we're Beer Geeks, not wine snobs) but also provide a very serious lineup of offerings. These two competing elements require a precarious balancing act.

When planning a beer tasting, a Beer Geek must seriously consider the following:

MARQUEE BOTTLE. The typical reason to host a beer tasting is to have an excuse to open a very special beer or collection of beers. It isn't essential, but a host is expected to have at least a few very VIP beers to open. A host should always strive not be outdone by his guests' beers, while a guest should attempt to bring a beer approaching, yet not exceeding, the quality of the host's marquee beer(s).

BOTTLE SHARE. While a Beer Geek may sometimes provide all or most of the beer (typically to make room in the cellar), more often than not, guests are also expected to bring beer to share.

INVITE LIST. The level of a guest's geekiness should be appropriate to the beers being poured. Guests selected should be able to appreciate the rarity and specialness of the marquee bottle(s).

THEME. A tasting needs direction and should therefore have a central theme. Be it a style (barrel-aged imperial stouts), a brewery, or a level of rarity, a theme provides cohesiveness and flow.

THE INVITATION. The invitation should clearly convey that the event is a beer tasting. While a BBQ or ugly sweater theme could be combined with the tasting, it is important that invitees understand that the foremost activity will be tasting and analyzing world-class beers. Having a party of another kind and attempting to simultaneously hold a beer tasting is a disservice to the beer. Spouses and significant others should always be invited (no need to make being a Beer Geek more difficult). However, if the significant other is not a Beer Geek, he or she should understand that this is a tasting and not mock the event or complain of boredom. Finally, the invitation should clearly state the serving format as well as the quantity, caliber, and style of beers that guests are expected to bring.

OPENING METHOD AND SERVING FORMAT

While serving beer at a tasting may seem simple, much thought should be given to determine the ideal serving format. Consider the type of beer as well as the crowd, and choose from the following formats:

PASS THE BOTTLE. The most common, but one of the most inefficient serving methods. The group sits around a table, and bottles are opened and passed around for everyone to fill his or her glass. A key disadvantage is that the group can imbibe only as fast as the slowest drinker, creating party-stalling issues. To be avoided.

VERTICAL. The opening of sequential vintages of the same beer. Usually, three years are opened at once to sustain a relatively constant serving temperature for comparison purposes. Each vintage should be provided with a separate glass, and all glassware should be similar, again for comparison purposes. Hosting a vertical tasting speaks to one's long-term dedication as a Beer Geek, though it can be a bit bittersweet for the host after the years of preparation.

BLIND TASTING. Various beers of the same style are served without the tasters knowing what they are drinking. Generally unpopular with Beer Geeks, as it diminishes the flavor of rarity. Ideally, the pouring should be done by teetotaling or pregnant attendees (so that all participants can be "blind") but is otherwise the responsibility of the host. A blind tasting is often done in the hopes of proving that a Beer Geek's local option can go toe-to-toe with the big guns of the national scene. If successful, a social media campaign is launched by attendees to inform the world of the results (refer to The Great Hype Machine, page 111).

TABLE TASTING. The standard Beer Geek tasting approach. Various bottles are opened concurrently (quantity dependent on strength of beer and number of tasters) and placed on a table. Attendees can sample at will, and the host opens new beers as bottles are finished. This classic format accommodates varying drinking rates, preferences, and pour sizes.

ME FIRST. Essentially the same as table tasting except that bottles are opened by the person who brought them. The bottle's owner first serves himself and then puts the remainder of the bottle on the share table. This method generally encourages tasters to bring higher-quality beer, since they won't be afraid of getting just a few ounces of their personal whale.

HIGH ROLLER (OR McAFEE). Another variation of table tasting with the key addition of a timer. Table tasting can often get stalled by beers that no one wants to finish. In a high-roller tasting, the bottle is opened, and a timer is set (usually for 30 minutes). Any beer left unfinished when the timer goes off is poured down the drain, and a new set of bottles is opened. The timer is restarted, and the process begins again. While this may seem wasteful, in reality, little beer ends up being poured out since the tasters are aware of its impending fate.

RANDOM-ASS OPENING. The worst kind of opening method, which results when there is a lack of direction. Bottles are opened at random, at random times, and by random people. Many beers are not finished, and many tasters leave disappointed because they missed out on beers they had wanted to try. The domain of noobs.

THE PERFECT HOST

Now that you have planned the perfect tasting, don't forget to be the perfect host. During the tasting, be sure to keep the following in mind to ensure those lovely beers get their due:

SETTLING TIME. Many beers (lambics and vintage beers) often have a collection of sediment in the bottom of the bottle, particularly if they have been laid on their side. Allow at least a few hours for these beers to settle after they are purchased or brought from the cellar. If being served from a lambic basket, the beers should be allowed to settle in the basket.

TEMPERATURE. Beers that have spent extended time in the fridge need time to warm to proper serving temperature prior to serving. Likewise, beers that warmed on the journey to the tasting must be given time to cool. Be sure to allot adequate space in the refrigerator.

REFRIGERATOR CONTENTS. Beer not intended for consumption at the tasting should be removed from the refrigerator to avoid confusion. However, top-tier beers should be prominently displayed (and readily opened) to show the caliber of one's cellar.

PACE. You are responsible for the pace of the tasting. While drunken-pirate speed isn't necessary, it should be quick enough so that no one is ever wanting for a new beer.

Finally, as the tasting winds down, the host ensures that everyone has a ride home and cabs are called as necessary. After the last guest leaves, all empty bottles are lined up on the tasting table, and a picture is posted to Facebook to inform the world that the greatest tasting ever has just occurred.

Beer Tasting Necessities

1. **GLASSWARE:** Roughly two glasses should be provided per taster, both to move things along and to provide the opportunity to compare two beers side by side. The type of glass should be appropriate to the style of beer being served. If necessary, it is acceptable to ask guests to bring their own glassware.

2. **RINSE WATER:** One pitcher of water for every four guests.

3. **DUMP BUCKET:** One large bowl centrally located for beers gone wrong.

4. **FOOD:** Meal-sized portions are not necessary, but snack foods should be provided. The food should not be so strongly flavored that it distracts from the beer (unless a beer and food pairing is planned). Plain breads and simple cheeses work very well.

5. **FRIDGE OR COOLER SPACE:** For guests' beers.

6. **PACER BEERS:** During tastings that involve very strong beers, a session lager provides welcome palate relief when drinking high-ABV or very potently flavored beers (sours, DIPAs, etc.).

7. **BOTTLE OPENER(S):** Both cork and cap openers should be strategically placed to avoid guests having to rummage through kitchen drawers.

8. **LAMBIC BASKET:** Holds beer at a 20-degree angle to make it easier to (somewhat) avoid pouring sediment from lambics and other sediment-laden beers. Empty tissue boxes make excellent lambic baskets.

9. **DECANTER:** Use when serving very old vintage beers.

CHAPTER 6
THE
BEERCATION
SEEKING THE SOURCE

An important rite of passage in a Beer Geek's life is to work through the Grand Tour of notable beer regions. While one could simply engage in beer trading to try these region-specific, difficult-to-procure beers, a Beer Geek is compelled to go to the source, soak in the terroir, and buy lots of authentic schwag to document that she has traveled across the world to drink a beer.

AS A RULE OF THUMB, the more difficult it is to get to your destination, the better the experience is. Extra points for visiting breweries whose beer is only available on-premises.

THE
MOTHERLAND

IN TERMS OF BEERCATIONS, Belgium is the pinnacle, the destination all others are compared against. The country holds a special place in Beer Geeks' hearts not just because the beer is delicious, but also because of the national reverence held for it. The way France respects wine, Belgium respects beer. Additionally, the transcontinental journey and associated cost settles any question of a Beer Geek's dedication to the craft.

Beer abounds everywhere in Belgium, so rather than seeking out good beer selections, you will simply be trying to separate the good from the excellent. In bars in the United States, you may occasionally have to settle on Budweiser; the Belgian "settle" beer is Duvel.

When visiting, an absolute must is the awkwardly titled but excellently written *Good Beer Guide Belgium*, by Tim Webb. The book is currently in its seventh edition, but bonus points are always awarded for toting around a well-used early version. New editions should be dog-eared and beer-stained at home prior to travel.

When in Belgium, a Beer Geek has two priorities:

1. finding beers to sample and enjoy while there, and

2. finding beers to bring back home.

Regarding the beers going in your luggage, the main focus should be on bottles that are not distributed to your home country, or at least are not easily found (Belgian lambics are a great example). This requires research prior to departure to ensure you know exactly what is and isn't available back home. There's nothing worse than lugging a beer halfway across the world only to find it sitting on a shelf at your local bottle shop.

While sizable books have been written on all the beery destinations, a Beer Geek hasn't really visited Belgium until he's ticked the following off his itinerary:

BRASSERIE CANTILLON. Chances are you'll be arriving in Belgium via **Brussels**, and any self-respecting Beer Geek will be found in Cantillon's taproom drinking some of the world's best lambic within an hour of exiting customs. Located just a few blocks from the centrally located Gare du Midi station, a €5 fee buys you a self-guided tour of some of the most Beer Geek–photographed brewing equipment in the world. Marvel at the random crates of whale-ish beers collecting dust in the hallway, and gaze at the walls of conditioning "loons" (Beer Geek slang for bottles of Cantillon). A flight of their cult-followed beers is included. Stock up on bottles, but do it on a second visit at the end of your trip to avoid lugging them across the country.

DRIE FONTEINEN. This stop is located in quaint **Beersel**, just a few miles outside of Brussels proper, but a world apart. The steepness of the hill between the Beersel train station and Drie Fonteinen is stuff of Beer Geek legend. The brewery and blending shop ooze lambic authenticity. Beers are typically poured and sold by the brewer/blender himself, Armand Debelder, providing Facebook photo gold. The bottle shop and tasting room are only open Fridays and Saturdays, a crucial logistical consideration. The attached restaurant (open Thursday through Monday) serves up fantastic dishes cooked with their world-class lambic, and their selection of vintage bottles and draft specialties will floor even the most jaded Beer Snob.

KULMINATOR. Located about an hour from Brussels in **Antwerp**, the Kulminator is arguably Belgium's best beer bar. Shoehorned into a thin slice of space on a random back street, it houses decades of cellared beers. A dictionary-sized beer menu includes anything from Trappist ales from the '70s to bottles of gueuze from long-lost lambic producers. At least a day should be dedicated to slowly exploring its vast selection.

CAFÉ 'T BRUGS BEERTJE. Located in picturesque **Brugge**, a town famous for medieval architecture, quaint canals, handmade lace, and roving gangs of umbrella-wielding Japanese tourists, this bar is famous not just for its outstanding beer list but also for its matronly proprietor Daisy Claeys. Her approving smile assures you that your beer order was a good one. Gorge yourself on the city's vast selection of chocolate and then spend a rainy day drinking in this national Belgian treasure.

IN DE VREDE. The café across the street from the Saint Sixtus Abbey, the monastery that brews the revered Westvleteren 12. While black-market "Westies" can be found in random beer bars and shops across the country, In De Vrede is the only place where it is reliably (and legally) available.

And while the monastery and brewery are not open to the public, just walking the grounds and absorbing its veneration is the way to properly enjoy these world-class brews. For the complete experience, the brewery should be approached on bike from nearby **Watou**. Completing the day with dinner at the world-famous beer restaurant the Hommelhof is a no-brainer.

Belgian Transportation

WHEN CHOOSING MODES OF TRANSPORTATION to travel across Belgium, consider that the more cumbersome the journey, the more authentic the experience. Using a car causes you to miss out on crucial cultural osmosis, and staying under the legal BAC limit of 0.05% makes for a very lame beercation indeed. A combination of trains and bikes are best. For the authentic Belgian beercation experience, a Beer Geek should receive at least one lift thanks to a newly formed friendship with a random Belgian bar patron or bartender.

EXPLORING THE **BELGIAN** COUNTRYSIDE

THE
FATHERLAND

RENOWNED FOR PERFECTING supremely drinkable beers, German beer is all about subtle elegance, not pushing the envelope. With no cult-followed breweries to hit or trade bait to stock up on, you can tour the beer regions of Germany knowing that you are telling the world that you are serious about beer and not just following the trends.

While non-Beer Geeks just think of pilsners and hefeweizens when they think of Germany, Beer Geeks know there is a vast array of other styles. The smoky rauchbier, the sweet yet powerful dopplebock, and the supremely drinkable kolsch are sometimes imitated by American breweries but very rarely equaled.

Each of these somewhat obscure styles originates from a specific region, having been tailored to local ingredients and brewing methods centuries ago. The draw of a German beercation is the opportunity to visit these regions and sample the wares of their centuries-old breweries. After trying the various versions of a specific German beer style, a Beer Geek has earned the right to authoritatively disparage any attempted imitation by a non-German brewery (it would only be snobby if it weren't true).

Germany's excellent rail system allows you to explore its numerous regions relatively quickly. To fully maximize the copious drinking opportunities, forget any silly notions of exploring castles or museums and instead just learn to shout, *"Bitte noch ein bier!"* (Another beer, please!).

MUNICH. First and foremost, the most important beer city of Germany. While noobs (and your aunt) will assume you will surely visit during Oktoberfest, Beer Geeks know that this 16-day festival is mostly a train wreck of rookies, vomit, and tourists and is best avoided. Brewery-dedicated beer halls abound throughout the city, as do quaint *biergartens*. Spend considerable time sampling the rich, bready Munich Dunkel. A showcase of what the Munich malt is capable of, this beer is rarely found — and never equaled — outside of the region. Also, don't miss Munich's clove-y yet fruity weissbier, which is what Americans know as hefeweizen.

BAMBERG. Though a Bavarian city, Bamberg manages to have a separate identity from the rest of Bavaria and is known for crafting kellerbiers (think cask-conditioned, Oktoberfest-style beers) and rauchbiers (also Oktoberfest-style, but brewed with beachwood-smoked malts). Kellerbiers are drunk out of hefty earthen mugs in local biergartens, making for one of the most enjoyable beer-drinking experiences a Beer Geek can have. The various rauchbiers vary in smokiness (light to full-on bacon) to fit almost any palate. The ultimate food beer, they have a lighter body well-suited to all-day sessioning. (To get an idea of this style, try the classic Aecht Schlenkerla rauchbier, which is distributed throughout the United States.) It's your cue to leave when your pee starts to smell smoky.

Oktoberfest

EACH OF THE SIX MAJOR GERMAN BREWERIES (Hofbrau, Lowenbrau, Hacker-Pschorr, Paulaner, Spaten/Franziskaner, and Augustiner) has a dedicated tent at this massive beer festival. Be prepared for your idea of an Oktoberfest beer to be a bit different from the style served. This "märzen" style beer is decidedly paler than the orangish Oktoberfest lagers found in the US and is designed for very high-volume swilling. Beers are served in one-liter mugs, so stomach-stretching exercises should be initiated well before traveling.

BERLIN. Not really a beer destination. However, since most will pass through here, Beer Geeks will certainly sample their regional style of beer, the Berliner weisse. Berliners know this unfiltered wheat beer soured by *Lactobacillus* as something drunk only by blue-haired grandmas and American Beer Geeks. It has otherwise been largely forgotten (or avoided) by the locals. To make it more approachable, it is traditionally served with sweet raspberry or woodruff (herbal green goo) syrup to reduce the sourness. A Beer Geek tries the syrup versions for the experience but otherwise drinks it straight (the bewildered look you receive from your bartender is part of the authentic experience). Unfortunately, after a steady market decline, the Berliner Kindl-Schultheiss is the only brewery that still regularly brews this stuff, though you can also find the mellower Bayerischer Bahnhof version from nearby **Leipzig**.

COLOGNE. A bustling medieval town with a rollicking beer scene, thanks in no small part to a large student population. The local beer is the kolsch and should not be confused with your local brewpub's "kolsch," which is really a corn-infused Bud Light substitute. Authentic kolsches are crisp, clean beers with delicate fruit notes, making them excellent session options. They are served in tall, narrow, 200-mL glasses called *stangens*, and servers wander the beer halls with racked trays, constantly replacing empty glasses. Over 20 local breweries offer their own versions, each with unique subtleties.

The German Viewpoint on Nonregional Beers

GERMANY IS KNOWN FOR its long-standing tolerance and acceptance of outsiders, but its stance on beer is a bit different. Germans are fiercely proud of their local region's beers, and most believe all other beers are varying degrees of garbage. The one exception seems to be Bavaria, whose beer receives begrudging admiration from the nation as a whole. In this same line of thinking, Bavarians themselves seem to think they brew the only beer worth drinking, though they have been known to make exceptions for a handful of non-Bavarian beers, like Rothaus Tannenzäpfle and Jever.

DUSSELDORF. At first glance, the city seems very business-oriented, but a quick visit to the Altstadt pedestrian walking mall along the Rhine reveals the city's fun side. The local altbier is a bitter, bronze brew balanced by a malty richness. An essential stop is the Uerige brewery to try their sticke alt, a slightly darker, thicker, and more powerful version of altbier that is the elixir of the beer gods.

....

BOCKS OF BAVARIA. Though they originated in the north German town of **Einbeck**, bocks are now best represented in the German free state of Bavaria. The bock style includes the light maibock, the powerful doppelbock, and the ice-distilled eisbock — all rich, malty lagers known for their strength and clean finish. Travel to Ayinger Brewery to try Celebrator, a doppelbock once hailed as the "world's best beer" by users of BeerAdvocate.com. Also make time to stop by the Kloster Andechs monastery, which has been brewing since 1455. Finally, check out Schneider Brewery, in **Kelheim**, and Kulmbacher Brewery, in **Upper Franconia**, to sample eisbocks, the German take on a barleywine.

BEERLANDIA

NEARLY 75 PERCENT OF AMERICAN-GROWN HOPS come from the Yakima Valley of Washington. A big chunk of the remaining portion are grown in Oregon's Willamette Valley, making these two neighboring states hotbeds for craft beer. And for a long time the Pacific Northwest was strictly for hop lovers. But there's more to life than just hops, and northwestern Beer Geeks began to develop a fondness for good beer in general, not just IPAs.

When touring the area, the obvious targets will be Portland and Seattle on the rainy western sides of the states, and Bend and Yakima in the drier agricultural area farther east. Before departing for the trip, male Beer Geeks should allow ample time to grow a respectable smattering of facial hair to assimilate with their Pacific Northwest brethren.

SEATTLE. The Emerald City is an excellent jumping-off point for a Beer Geek's Pacific Northwest tour. One of the first beercentric cities, for a while it was content living in its hoppy, grunge-rock past. New blood has emerged on the scene, though, and Seattle is once again ascending in glory. Beer Geeks should plan on spending an afternoon justifying their airline baggage fees at Bottleworks, one of the best bottle shops in the country. Also, Brouwer's Café is proving itself one of the best beer-food pairing spots in the world and is great for seducing non–Beer Geek spouses and significant others to the beery side of life. A visit to the under-the-radar Stumbling Monk, with its vintage rarities, provides abundant geek cred for Facebook glory.

YAKIMA. Beer Geeks take pride in visiting this decidedly blue-collar town, whose rough edges otherwise invite little to no tourism. A great overnight excursion from Seattle, Yakima is best visited in September when hop grower Hopunion hosts its annual Hop & Brew School. During this event some of the top brewers from across the country descend upon the town. You can tour the hop country by day and sample the goods with beer industry celebrities at night. Regardless of the time of year, Bale Breaker Brewing's beers and expansive grounds are always destination-worthy. **Note:** If traveling to or from Portland, a three-hour drive away, be sure to stop in **Hood River**, home to Full Sail and Beer Geek darling pFriem Family Brewers.

PORTLAND. Locals are well-known for their love of quality beer, so a Beer Geek will expend little effort finding quality suds in this city. The obvious first choice will be the Hair of the Dog taproom, where Beer Geeks won't bat an eye at their splurge-worthy vintage beer list. Respects are paid to Don Younger, the godfather of American Beer Geeks, whose Horse Brass Pub helped blaze the path for good beer in America. Score ridiculously rare take-home bottles at both the Cheese Bar and Woodstock Wine & Deli, two hidden gems. A stop at the Cascade Brewing Barrel House to sample its lactic-laced masterpieces is also a must. Local brewery chain McMenamins and its subpar beers should be avoided at all costs.

BEND. A three-hour drive from Portland, Bend seems like it could be located on the other side of the country. Sunny and dry, Bend is becoming a beer mecca, mostly due to the longtime presence of Deschutes Brewing, whose masterful beers have made the BMCs of the world an afterthought for many an Oregonian. Drink cult-worthy **hop bombs** at Boneyard Beer, and try some of the finest barrel-aged sour beers at The Ale Apothecary. Beer Geeks will take full advantage of Bend's relatively remote location to stock up on plenty of bragging schwag (get a knit hat if returning to Portland).

Airline Baggage Policy

ESSENTIALLY ALL US AIRLINES ALLOW BEER in their checked luggage, something Beer Geeks the country over take full advantage of when traveling. Beer can obviously be stored in your suitcase, but many Beer Geeks will instead opt to package and check their beer in a cardboard box picked up from a bottle shop. While clothes make for semi-decent packing material, their considerable weight cuts into the 50 allowed pounds, a detriment to the amount of beer you're planning on bringing home. Between this and the potential of having to pick glass shards out of a beer-drenched sweater, there is reason enough to regularly travel with bubble wrap or the like. Because two checked bags fly free, Southwest is the official airline of Beer Geeks everywhere.

THE
NAPA VALLEY
OF BEER

OFTEN, VACATIONS TO COLORADO do not start off as beercations. Instead, the mountains and their surrounding natural beauty lure outdoor enthusiasts in droves. However, anyone with any sort of beery inclination will quickly discover that the number of beercentric destinations in the Centennial State is an equally big, if not bigger, draw. Throw in the fact that the capital city of Denver hosts the Great American Beer Festival, and Colorado begins to look like the ultimate American beercation.

The beer destinations are centered in the three Front Range cities of Fort Collins, Boulder, and Denver. While they are less than an hour's drive from one another, the number of Beer Geek locales in each requires at least a day's dedicated work per city.

Unfortunately, with only a few exceptions, the nearby mountains are lacking in the beer department. The best approach is to stock up in the cities and bring a trunk full of beer up to the high country to accompany any outdoor adventure.

The overall Colorado scene is strong but mellow. There are very few breweries or beers produced in the state that have reached cult or whale status, but the overall volume and quality of beer brewed is second to none. Coloradans pride themselves in drinking good beer, and with even the most run-of-the-mill venues offering some sort of craft option, a Beer Geek will almost never have to settle for BMC.

DENVER. The biggest of these three beercentric cities, Denver used to lag behind its smaller brethren, but the local scene has surged in recent years. Be sure to visit the Falling Rock Tap House to sample from their deep cellar list. The largest craft brewery, Great Divide, is worth a stop, but the majority of Beer Geeks will zero in on cultish Crooked Stave, where owner Chad Yakobson, who did his masters in science dissertation on *Brettanomyces*, bends the wild yeast to his will. The grimy hidden gem of the city is Star Bar, a rundown dive bar with an affinity for crazy one-off sours from the likes of New Belgium, Avery, and Crooked Stave. Venturing up to the nearby hip Highlands neighborhood is rewarded by the ultra-impressive tap list at the pizza joint Hops & Pie.

BOULDER. The best place for Beer Geeks to stuff their suitcases, or car trunks, is the Boulder Liquor Mart with its seemingly endless beer coolers. Stop by Avery to check out taproom exclusives, as well as FATE Brewing, which is proving to be best-in-class among the new wave of breweries. Odd13 in nearby **Lafayette** is a local's favorite due to their dedication to barrel-aging and a deft hand with the hops. Top restaurant beer spots are Backcountry Pizza & Tap House and the West End Tavern. Earn extra vacation cash by donning a tye-dyed hemp poncho and playing the drums on empty beer boxes on the Pearl Street Mall.

FORT COLLINS. The city that put Colorado on the Beer Geek map. The combination of stalwarts New Belgium and Odell with avant-garde Funkwerks and Equinox make Fort Collins a powerhouse of a beer city. Brewery visits have to include these four, which can all be hit on one 2.5-mile urban "hike" using the city's dedicated walking path. Also, venture out to see some of the newly opened operations, Black Bottle being the strongest of the bunch. Restaurant and beer bar options abound, but at a minimum, hit Mayor of Old Town and Choice City Butcher & Deli.

THE MOUNTAINS. The biggest beercentric draw of the mountains will be the Big Beers, Belgians & Barleywines Festival held each January in **Vail**. This festival, which requires all beer poured to be over 8% ABV or Belgian in origin draws celebrity-level brewers looking to drink quality suds while enjoying some of the best skiing in the country (rubbing elbows with Sam Calagione or Tomme Arthur is commonplace). Until recently, the mountains of Colorado didn't hold any Beer Geek gold, but Casey Brewing & Blending, opened in **Glenwood Springs** in 2013, has changed things up. Focusing only on barrel-aged sours made from in-state ingredients (including fruit), this brewery has quickly developed a cult following. Backcountry Brewery in **Frisco** is also a good road trip stop off of I-70.

NORTHERN CALIFORNIA

CHICO.
RUSSIAN RIVER
•SANTA ROSA
BERKELEY
•SAN FRANCISCO

CALIFORNIA

PASO ROBLES
•KERNVILLE
BUELLTON
LOS ANGELES
SAN MARCOS
•ESCONDIDO
•SAN DIEGO

BEACHES AND BREWS

WHILE IN MOST STATES the destination-worthy breweries are found in and around the major cities, high rent prices have driven most California breweries to little out-of-the-way towns, removed from the sprawling metropolises. The legwork of trekking far from major airports, however, just serves to whet a Beer Geek's pallet.

Because the amount of time spent visiting beer destinations in the Golden State can be extensive, it's best to focus a Cali beercation on a particular region of the state. For the most part, this means flying into San Francisco and exploring Northern California, or flying into San Diego to roam the southern portion. But there are also a few areas in between that are worth a Beer Geek's time.

SAN FRANCISCO. Practically devoid of breweries (Cellarmaker being the notable exception), this port city nonetheless has a very solid beer bar scene. The stronghold is Toronado, a dive bar with an epic vintage list. Bottles are available to go, and their beer list almost always includes über-fresh Pliny the Elder. This small bar is so highly regarded that Russian River blended special beers to commemorate its 20th and 25th anniversaries — both beers are considered white whales. Also worth checking out is Mikkeller Bar in the Tenderloin district, where the selection is exactly what you'd expect from a man who has built an empire by catering to Beer Geeks' whims.

NORTHERN CALIFORNIA. After a quick stop at The Rare Barrel brewery in **Berkeley**, any Beer Geek heading north of San Francisco is certainly headed straight for Russian River Brewing Company in **Santa Rosa**. One of the ultimate Beer Geek breweries, the tap list at its brewpub is always stellar. The signature genie-bottle-shaped growler makes for an excellent bragging prop when being filled back home. (And the fact that Santa Rosa is nestled in the heart of Sonoma wine country makes a great combo for Beer Geeks with wine-loving spouses.) On the way to Russian River, Lagunitas Brewing Company is a favorite stop. A bit further north is **Chico**, home of Sierra Nevada Brewing, and to the west is both the ocean and North Coast Brewing, where you can find amazing barrel-aged versions of their imperial beers.

SAN DIEGO. Home to some of the most respected breweries in America, the hills surrounding San Diego are a Beer Geek mecca. Stone Brewing started it all, and their World Bistro and Gardens in **Escondido** is certainly the most beautiful brewery taproom in the United States. Essentially a botanical garden combined with an exceptional restaurant and a world-class beer list (including many guest taps), a visit here will make your entire trip worthwhile. Nearby, The Lost Abbey in **San Marcos** is an essential stop, making any Beer Geek's luggage about 50 pounds heavier upon departure. Closer to the city, drop into Ballast Point, Green Flash, and AleSmith breweries, which only add to the area's epicness. Last but not least, to the east of the city is Alpine Beer Company, probably the largest draw of the area for most Beer Geeks. They have a way with hops that makes them the gold standard of the West Coast hop style.

CENTRAL CALIFORNIA. In reality, a beercation is never going to be made of the Central Valley of the state. However, there are a few draws to cause a Beer Geek to consider extending her Northern or Southern California beercation. The most notable is Firestone Walker in rural **Paso Robles**. Their double mastery of sours and big barrel-aged beers (Parabola and Sucaba, for example) has won over Beer Geeks from coast to coast. Depending on the direction you're coming from, Firestone Walker's other facility, Barrelworks, in **Buellton** provides an alternative way to stock up and try the goodies as well. The other alluring locale is Kern River Brewing Company in **Kernville**, whose Citra Double IPA has jet-setting Beer Geeks flying in from all over the world for its release (seriously).

LOS ANGELES. Visit The Bruery, visit Beachwood Brewing, and then jump in your car and don't stop driving until you reach San Diego.

LEAF PEEPING AND BEER DRINKING

MENTION THE EAST COAST (anywhere outside of the beer world) and immediately people think of New York, Boston, and Philadelphia. And while these massive cities certainly have their own respectable beer scenes, most Beer Geeks won't consider them destination-worthy. No, when Beer Geeks think of visiting the East Coast, the small "farm country" breweries of New England are what come to mind.

Mostly due to antiquated brewery-friendly laws, the small states of New England are littered with tiny breweries focused on making beer for their surrounding community. Much like wine-loving visitors of the boutique wineries of California, Beer Geeks love to tour the countryside and visit the renowned breweries with cult followings as well as discover new ones. For Beer Geeks whose significant others don't share their beery passion, this serves as an excellent destination when combined with the fall activity of gazing at leaves. Non–beer drinkers also serve as excellent designated drivers (bonus), as most destinations are reachable only by car.

VERMONT. The foremost New England state when it comes to beer, the Green Mountain State is best known for two breweries: Hill Farmstead and The Alchemist. Hill Farmstead, located in sleepy **Greensboro Bend**, is the brainchild of Shaun Hill, who decided to turn his grandfather's farmhouse into what has become one of the world's most highly regarded breweries. To wait in line to fill one of their growlers is to earn a Beer Geek badge of honor. Meanwhile, The Alchemist, just a little over an hour away in **Waterbury**, is famous for making the long-reigning #1 beer in the world, Heady Topper (per BeerAdvocate.com ratings). Be sure to sample and stock up on this hoppy delight (which is essentially the default beer-trading currency), but also check out the other equally awesome beers, which can only be had on the premises. In addition to these two breweries, Beer Geeks have to visit the Saturday Farmers Market in **Waitsfield**, as this is best way to buy beers from Lawson's Finest Liquids, another cult-followed brewery.

MAINE. You know you are a Beer Geek if you are aware that Ebenezer's Pub, a tiny bar-restaurant located inside a barn in the itty-bitty town of **Lovell**, houses arguably the best beer cellar in the entire nation (if not the world). Beer Geeks plan entire trips around visiting this nondescript locale and rarely leave disappointed (so long as it's actually open). In addition to Ebenezer's, the state also boasts Maine Brewing Company, a little brewery in **Freeport** known for making small-batch hoppy delights, and Allagash, the **Portland**-based maker of Belgian-style ales whose beers often rival those they set out to copy.

MASSACHUSETTS. Though Vermont can lay the most claim to creating the New England IPA renaissance, it's now Massachusetts that is doing a lot of the legwork to carry that ultra-popular torch. In **Boston**, check out Trillium, a young brewery known for its mastery of all things hoppy, before ending the evening at Lord Hobo, a beer bar with one of the most well-chosen draft lists in the country. Head east on I-90 for about 30 minutes to visit Jack's Abby in **Framingham**, the brewery that let America know that lagers can be so much more than yellow, fizzy swill. Another hour down I-90 will lead to hop-mastermind Tree House Brewing in **Monson**, where you should fill as many growlers as your trunk will allow.

THOSE OTHER STATES. Other beer highlights include Portsmouth Brewery in **New Hampshire**, made famous through the adoration of the Alström Bros (founders of BeerAdvocate). The entire town of **Portsmouth** is beer-crazy and a great place to spend a day. If passing through **Connecticut**, New England Brewing Company in **Woodbridge**, famous for its Fuzzy Baby Ducks IPA, also boasts a bevy of excellent non-hoppy options. In Rhode Island . . . there is a fantastically clean rest stop at Exit 8 off I-95.

BEERYMOONS AND BEER GEEK WEDDINGS
CONSUMMATING YOUR GEEKINESS

RELATIONSHIPS ARE OFTEN FORMED through mutual interests and loves, so it's no surprise that many Beer Geeks end up dating and sometimes even tie the knot. For those lucky enough to end up in this situation, the desire to integrate craft beer into the big day is clearly mutual.

Many Beer Geek couples celebrate beercentric weddings by holding the reception at a brewery, having hop-and-barley corsages and boutonnières, using barleywine at communion, or adding other creative touches. While this is all well and good, a Beer Geek's main responsibility involves the beer offerings at the reception.

Wedding receptions are one of the last bastions of BMC dominance, and getting good craft options can sometimes be difficult and require persistence. A wedding should be a celebration of the couple, however, and what's served to family and friends is a reflection of them as a couple. Therefore, good craft beer must be available. That being said,

... a Beer Geek recognizes that a wedding is not the time to convince Uncle Merle to ditch the Labatts, and there is no shame in making BMC concessions to those who have yet to see the light.

An estimate should be made of the craft-appreciating crowd, and the variety and quantity ordered should err on the side of "better too much than too little," be it a case of SNPA or three kegs of Half Acre's Daisy Cutter.

Finally, the climax of the event: the wedding toast. For this historic moment, a Beer Geek couple goes for the gold. The toasting liquid should be thoroughly considered and fastidiously chosen. Boon's Oude Geuze Mariage Parfait is always a classy choice.

Many recently married Beer Geek couples choose to forgo the traditional honeymoon in favor of a beercentric one, referred to as a **beerymoon**. These trips are a bit different from your average beercations because the emphasis is partly on unwinding from all the craziness of the wedding and not solely focused on drinking world-class brews. Consider it a win-win: after you finish sleeping in and getting massages, the beer's there waiting for you.

A Beer Geek's Champagne Toast

PATIENCE IS A VIRTUE
BEING THE SPOUSE / SIGNIFICANT OTHER
OF A BEER GEEK

By Lindsay Dawson

IF YOU'RE READING THIS SECTION, you're likely either the spouse/significant other of a Beer Geek or someone who suspects they might be the spouse/significant other of a Beer Geek. Whichever it is,

. . . welcome. This is a safe place.

Being the spouse or significant other of a Beer Geek is no easy feat. In fact, I'm going to say that at times it's a damn art. It's not that we don't support our Beer Geek's obsess — *ahem*, interests. On the contrary, I'm sure that you, like me, would much rather your beloved spend time and money on beer instead of something like, say, strip clubs (and yes, this can apply whether your geek is male or female). At the same time, when you begin to find that the majority of your geek's thoughts, conversations, e-mails, errands, texts, to-do lists, gifts, vacations . . . are trending beerward, it can require of you an extra helping of loving patience.

Lucky for you, I've experienced just about all there is to experience when it comes to having a Beer Geek mate, and I've come out on the other side. So I write the following as both a friendly heads up and an empathetic pat on the back.

(**Quick note:** for simplicity's sake, I'll henceforth refer to the Beer Geek as "BG" and spouse or significant other as "BS," since that's what we often have to put up with — kidding, kidding.)

For those of you who have been married to or dated the same person for at least a little while, you're already well aware if they're a BG. So to you, I dedicate an especially heartfelt pat on the back. However, for those of you who are in a relatively new relationship and are still a little unsure about whether or not you have an actual BG on your hands, the following should not only help answer the question but also alert you to some of the common BG nuances you can expect to encounter. ("A chilled pint glass?! What, do they not want me to taste *anything*?")

So here we go. For all you BSs (or potential BSs) out there:

YOU KNOW YOU'VE GOT A BG ON YOUR HANDS IF . . .

- The food in your fridge is slowly, but surely, edged out. Pretty soon you've got eggs replaced by eisbocks, salsa exchanged for sours, porters instead of pickles, and lambics for leftovers. Hope you like drinking your meals.

- Black Friday is stressful, but it's not because of the deals on electronics. Ohhhh, no. It's BCBS Strategy Day. Batten down the hatches, because it's go-time.

- Your conversation at a liquor store goes something like this:

  BS: *Ooh, look, babe! Pliny's finally back on the shelf. You've been waiting for it, right?*

  BG: *Sweet!! Oh, wait, never mind . . .*

  BS: *What's wrong? The price isn't bad. Grab a couple.*

  BG: *Why bother? It was bottled three days ago. The hops are all gone . . .*

  BS: [silence]

- The terms *vertical* and *whale* are mentioned and the last thing that comes to mind is a direction and a mammal.

- You know it's pronounced *can-tee-yOHn.*

- You understand that the most crucial aspect of a beer trade isn't how well-packaged the beer is to survive the travel, but what beers are chosen as the "extras." *(Sweet mother of %$#@, you don't want to hear about it if they screw this one up.)*

- Gone are the days of beer-tasting comments such as, "Yep, this beer tastes good. I like the flavor." Now it's, "Cardboard! I taste CARDBOARD!!" and, "The head retention disturbs me."

- Your BG's question before even sitting down at a bar is, "Yeah, you got a Reserve list?"

- Your upcoming vacation to France inspires a conversation like this:

    BS: *I can't believe we're going to the south of France! I'm so excited. And driving's such a good way to see the countryside.*

    BG: *Yeah, me too. You know . . . if we took the scenic route, we could swing through Brussels on the way and hit up Cantillon.*

    BS: *On the way to what? Brussels is ten hours to the north.*

    BG: [silence/averts eyes]

    BS: [questioning look]

    BG: [silence/averts eyes]

- A beer tasting between your BG and one of his or her buddies might sound something akin to this:

    BG 1: *Yeah, it's fine and all. It's just drinking a little young.*

    BG 2: *It's one of only five left in the world.*

    BG 1: *I mean, I love it.*

I can practically hear you shaking your head and sighing in an "I know it all too well" manner. To you, I offer this assurance: hang in there, we're in this together. For those of you who, upon reading this, knew deep down that it sounded familiar (*heavy sigh; pat, pat, pat*) . . . you, my friend, have a certified BG on your hands.

So don't worry when you find yourself having difficulty remaining calm when everyone at the table's ready to order their drinks and your BG is calculating whether a 10-oz. pour of that barleywine is as good a deal as the 12-oz. double IPA. Take a deep breath, and know you're not alone. And if you find yourself needing a bit of additional support, keep in mind the following mantra: *Patience, love, understanding. I'm a good person. I love my BG. Patience, love, understanding* . . . (That, and you might want to invest in a kickboxing class.)

Welcome to the club . . . and good luck.

THE BEER GEEK
DICTIONARY

As you know by now, Beer Geeks love to talk (and write) about beer. And, as with almost every industry or hobby, a special set of vocabulary has emerged. For example, if a beer is called "sessionable," a Beer Geek immediately knows that it's under 5% alcohol, has a light body, is low in residual sugars, and lends itself to being consumed in large quantities. Vocabulary such as this not only increases communication efficiency, it also acts as a signal to other Beer Geeks that you are in the know.

To not appear a noob, it is important to recognize and understand this specialized jargon, something achieved only through intense immersion in beer websites, books, and conversations. Much of Beer Geek slang comes and goes, but there is a certain baseline vocabulary that all Beer Geeks should know, lest they have no idea what the discussion is about.

* indicates an acronym that can be spoken as letters, unless otherwise specified (most are written, not said)

3F: Drie Fonteinen

ABV: Alcohol By Volume

AFTW: Adam from the Wood, brewed by Hair of the Dog Brewery

BA: Barrel-aged, or BeerAdvocate.com, the website

BARNYARD: A flavor descriptor for the earthy, funky flavors found in lambics and some other *Brettanomyces*-brewed beers

BCBS: Bourbon County Brand Stout, brewed by Goose Island Beer Co.

BCBCS: Bourbon County Brand Coffee Stout, brewed by Goose Island Beer Co. Also referred to simply as "Coffee"

BCS: Black Chocolate Stout, brewed by Brooklyn Brewery

BEERCATION: A vacation centered around drinking regional beers and experiencing the local beer culture

BEERYMOON: A honeymoon beercation

BIF: Beer It Forward, a type of group beer trade

BMC: Stands for Bud-Miller-Coors, but really refers to any factory-manufactured, yellow, fizzy lager, regardless of producer

BOMBER: A 22-oz. bottle of beer

BRETT: *Brettanomyces*, a wild yeast

CBS: Canadian Breakfast Stout

CCB: Cigar City Brewing

CLOYING: A syrupy-sweet texture. Typically a negative feature

DDG: Duck Duck Gooze, brewed by The Lost Abbey

DECOCTION MASHING: Repeatedly boiling wort to produce a rich, kettle-caramelized malt character

DOMING: The act of drinking a bottle of beer by oneself (usually a very large, or rare, high-ABV bottle)

DONG: Draft only, no growlers (pronounced "DONG," not "D-O-N-G")

DRAIN POUR: An exceptionally bad beer

ELDER: Pliny the Elder, brewed by Russian River Brewing Co.; see also *PtE*

FFF: Three Floyds Brewing Co.

FFTW: Fred from the Wood, brewed by Hair of the Dog Brewery

FT: For trade

FW: Firestone Walker Brewing Co.

GABF: Great American Beer Festival

GHOST WHALE: The rarest of white whales

GIF: Growler It Forward, a type of group beer trade

GLASSWALE: A very rare beer glass

GROWLER: A refillable 64-oz. glass beer container. Typically filled at the brewery, though some states allow off-premises fills

HANDBOTTLE: A DONG that has been poured into a resealable bottle for beer-trading purposes

HEADY: Heady Topper, brewed by The Alchemist

HF: Hill Farmstead Brewery

HOP BOMB: A very hop-forward beer

HOT: Having a strong alcohol flavor and presence

HOTD: Hair of the Dog Brewing Company

HUNA: Hunahpu's Imperial Stout, brewed by Cigar City Brewing

IBU: International Bittering Units. A measure of hop bitterness in a beer

IP: In person, (in reference to beer trading), or Isabelle Proximus, brewed by The Lost Abbey

ISO: In search of

'KBS: Kentucky Breakfast Stout, brewed by Founders

LA: The Lost Abbey

LIF: Lottery It Forward, a type of group beer trade

LOON: A beer brewed by Cantillon

LP: Lou Pepe, a series of beers brewed by Cantillon

MAB: A one-liter, dimpled German beer hall mug (pronounced "mahss")

MOAS: Mother of All Storms, brewed by Pelican Brewery

MOUTHFEEL: The sensation of a beer's flavor (viscous, metallic, warming, prickly, etc.)

NIP: A small (typically 9-oz.) bottle of beer

NOOB: A derogatory term for someone who displays a lack of beer knowledge

ONE-OFF: A beer made only once, as opposed to a regular lineup beer

PTE: Pliny the Elder, brewed by Russian River Brewing Co.; see also *Elder*

PTY: Pliny the Younger, brewed by Russian River Brewing Co.

RARE: Bourbon County Brand Stout Rare, brewed by Goose Island Beer Co.

RR: Russian River Brewing Co.

SESSION BEER: A low-ABV (less than 4.5% or 5%, depending who you ask) beer designed to be consumed continually for an extended period of time

SHELF TURD: Usually good but overpriced beer that sits on store shelves for a long period of time. Often used sarcastically

SNPA: Sierra Nevada Pale Ale

TICKER/TICK: A ticker is a beer drinker who focuses on drinking only rare beers and only one time each. A tick is a beer drunk by a ticker.

WESTY: Westvleteren Trappist Brewery or its beer

WHALE/WALE/WALEZ: An incredibly rare, sought-after beer

WHITE WHALE: The rarest of whales

WORT: The sweet liquid extracted during the mashing process of brewing beer; the sugars in the wort ferment to produce alcohol

YOUNGER: Pliny the Younger, brewed by Russian River Brewing Co.; see also *PtY*

Commonly Mispronounced Beer Names and Terms

BEATIFICATION = be-at-i-fah-KAY-shun

CANTILLON = cahn-tee-YHON

DRIE FONTEINEN = dree-fawn-TAY-nen

DUVEL = DOO-vul (Flemish speakers) or doo-VELL (French speakers)

FARO = FAH-row

FRAMBOISE = fhrom-BWAZ

GOSE = GOES-zuh

GUEUZE/GEUZE = g'hurz (French speakers) or g'khghrys-gkr-zuh (Flemish speakers)

HUNAHPU = HOO-nah

JAI ALAI = hi-li

LAGUNITAS = lah-goo-NEE-tuss

PIRAAT = PEE-raht

PLINY = PLY-nee (plin-ee is the historical figure)

ROCHEFORT = ROWSH-fhor

SMITHWICKS = SMID-icks

SUCABA = AB-ah-cuss

WESTVLETEREN = vest-FLAY-tren

WESTMALLE = VEST-mall-uh

WEIHENSTEPHANER = gvhen-STEF-on-ee

YUENGLING = YING-ling

MORE BOOKS FOR BEER GEEKS

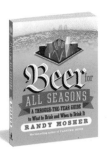

John Holl

Beer writer John Holl visited 900 brewpubs and taverns across the United States to collect the best beer-friendly recipes. Augment your craft beer experience with dishes like Roasted Chipotle Salsa Burgers or Crawfish Bordelaise.

Randy Mosher

This delicious and extensive guide to beer and beer festivals all over the world, organized by season, will help you pick the best beers for any climate and occasion.

Alan D. Eames

Educate yourself with this fun collection of cultural history, legends, lore, little-known facts, and quirky quotes by beer drinkers from Nietzsche to Darwin.

Patrick Dawson

Learn how to identify a cellar-worthy beer, how to set up a beer cellar, what to look for when tasting vintage beers, and the fascinating science behind the aging process.

 Storey Publishing